PLOUGHSHARES

Winter 2004–05 · Vol. 30, No. 4

GUEST EDITOR
Joy Harjo

EDITOR
Don Lee

MANAGING EDITOR
Gregg Rosenblum

POETRY EDITOR
David Daniel

ASSOCIATE FICTION EDITOR
Maryanne O'Hara

FOUNDING EDITOR
DeWitt Henry

FOUNDING PUBLISHER
Peter O'Malley

PLOUGHSHARES, a journal of new writing, is guest-edited serially by prominent writers who explore different and personal visions, aesthetics, and literary circles. PLOUGHSHARES is published in April, August, and December at Emerson College, 120 Boylston Street, Boston, MA 02116-4624. Telephone: (617) 824-8753. Web address: www.pshares.org.

ASSISTANT FICTION EDITORS: Jay Baron Nicorvo and Nicole Kelley. EDITORIAL ASSISTANTS: Shannon Miller and Elizabeth E. Partfitt. BOOKSHELF ADVISORS: Fred Leebron and Cate Marvin. PROOFREADER: Megan Weireter.

FICTION READERS: Kathleen Rooney, Christopher Helmuth, Eson Kim, Simeon Berry, Dan Medeiros, Leslie Busler, Erin Lavelle, Maureen Cidzik, Jessica Keener, Matthew Modica, Wendy Wunder, Cortney Hamilton, Emily Ekle, Hannah Bottomy, Ashley Joseph O'Shaughnessy, Asako Serizawa, James Charlesworth, Patricia Reed, Leslie Cauldwell, Joanna Luloff, Scarlett Stoppa, Megan Weireter, Tammy Zambo, Sara Whittleton, Emily Santolla, and Marin Buschel. POETRY READERS: Kathleen Rooney, Simeon Berry, Autumn McClintock, Zachary Sifuentes, Christopher Tonelli, Elisa Gabbert, Erin Lavelle, Tracy Gavel, Jennifer Thurber, and Robert Arnold.

SUBSCRIPTIONS (ISSN 0048-4474): $24 for one year (3 issues), $46 for two years (6 issues); $27 a year for institutions. Add $12 a year for international ($10 for Canada).

UPCOMING: Spring 2005, a poetry and fiction issue edited by Martín Espada, will appear in April 2005. Fall 2005, a fiction issue edited by Antonya Nelson, will appear in August 2005.

SUBMISSIONS: Reading period is from August 1 to March 31 (postmark dates). All submissions sent from April to July are returned unread. Please see page 199 for editorial and submission policies.

Back-issue, classroom-adoption, and bulk orders may be placed directly through PLOUGHSHARES. Microfilms of back issues may be obtained from University Microfilms. PLOUGHSHARES is also available as CD-ROM and full-text products from EBSCO, H.W. Wilson, Information Access, and UMI. Indexed in M.L.A. Bibliography, American Humanities Index, Index of American Periodical Verse, Book Review Index. Full publisher's index is online at www.pshares.org. The views and opinions expressed in this journal are solely those of the authors. All rights for individual works revert to the authors upon publication.

PLOUGHSHARES receives support from the National Endowment for the Arts and the Massachusetts Cultural Council.

Retail distribution by Ingram Periodicals and Bernhard DeBoer. Printed in the U.S.A. on recycled paper by Capital City Press.

CONTENTS

Winter 2004–05

Ploughshares Patrons

This nonprofit publication would not be possible without the support of our readers and the generosity of the following individuals and organizations. Please see the next page for an additional list of subscriber donations.

COUNCIL
William H. Berman
Denise and Mel Cohen
Robert E. Courtemanche
Jeff and Jan Greenhawt
Jacqueline Liebergott
Turow Foundation
Eugenia Gladstone Vogel
Marillyn Zacharis

PATRON
Johanna Cinader

FRIENDS
Anonymous (2)
Robert Hildreth
Drs. Jay and Mary Anne Jackson
Tom Jenks and Carol Edgarian
Patrick O'Brien
Christopher and Colleen Palermo
Robert A. Silverman
L. C. Wisnewski

ORGANIZATIONS
Emerson College
Lannan Foundation
Massachusetts Cultural Council
National Endowment for the Arts

COUNCIL: $3,000 for two lifetime subscriptions and acknowledgement in the journal for three years.
PATRON: $1,000 for a lifetime subscription and acknowledgement in the journal for two years.
FRIEND: $500 for a lifetime subscription and acknowledgement in the journal for one year.

Ploughshares Donors

With great gratitude, we would like to acknowledge the following
subscribers who generously made donations to
Ploughshares during 2004.

Anonymous (24)
Kim Addonizio
Heidi Arnold
Mary Jo Bang
George Blecher
Jill Bossert
Judy Brand
Alice Byers
Criss E. Cannady
Robert E. Cetlin, Ph.D.
Nancy Christopherson
Faus Geiger Corlett
Janet S. Crossen
Saralyn R. Daly
Robert F. Derenthal
Douglas W. Downey
Stuart Dybek
Paula Eder
Lawrence Feldman
Ted R. Frame
George Garrett
Norton R. Girault
Teja W. Geldmacher
Leilani R. Hall
Thomas Hanold
Ethan Hauser
Judith Higgins
Houghton Mifflin Co.
Kristen R. Kish
Joseph Kostolefsky
Frank Kramer
   Harvard Book Store
Maxine Kumin

Linda Levin-Scherz
David Leviten
Harold and Edith Lohr
Cynthia Macdonald
Betty Keneipp Marsh
Maile Meloy
Helaine Miller
Jeanne Morrel-Franklin
Neil and Jane Pappalardo
Rod Parker
Patricia Polak
Julianne Powers
Jennie Rathbun
Shannon Ravenel
Jennifer Rose
Ken and Barbara Rosenblum
Joan P. Scherer
Tim Seibles
Carol Houck Smith
Nat Sobel
Debra Spark
Maura Stanton
Synapse Group
Barbara Tran
Nigel Twose
Richard F. Vincent
Dick Vittitow
Ellen Bryant Voigt
Rosanna Warren
Joan M. Wendling
Charlotte A. Williams
Tobias Wolff
C. Stuart Wright

JOY HARJO

Introduction

I used to think a poem could become a flower, a bear, or a house for a ravaged spirit. I used to think I understood what it meant to write a poem, and understood the impetus to write, and even knew a little something of the immensity of the source of poetry. I was never the scholar and approached the study of poetry like a fool in love with the moon. I mean, I am a reader of poetry and know a little something about the various indigenous roots of American poetry. I know even more about European elements of verse, because it was all we were taught in public schools, hammered as the "truly civilized poetry." I had to stand quite a distance from the earth, beyond conquest politics, to see the foolishness of this assertion. To say one form of poetry ranks above all others is to insist on a hierarchy of value that arbitrarily rules that a rose has more value than an orchid because it is a rose.

It was in song that I first found poetry, or it found me, alone at the breaking of dawn under the huge elm sheltering my childhood house, within range of the radio, of my mother's voice. I used to think that the elm, too, was poetry, as it expressed the seasonal shifts and rooted us. Ever since, I have given myself over to poetry. Poetry, like the earth, was once decreed flat, then round. I declare it as a spiral in shape and movement. Each strand of poetry curls from classical form and springs unruly forms that often overtake and become classical forms as the tendrils of songs coil into the future.

I used to think a story would house a beginning, middle, and end and could be contained within the covers of a book, then given a home in the heart. Or that a story in any of its forms could lead me safely away from myself, show me a world so different I would return to gaze at my known universe with a newly shining mind. I believed that myth was alive and was the mothering source of stories, poetry, and songs, and within this field I would find the provocative answers to the riddle of being a human without wings or gills, or directions to a map for a lost wanderer. I was looking for vision, for the powerful and startling and subtle strategies of language, pattern, style, character, and voice that would satisfy and, even more, inspire. I have given myself over to the making of stories, and even as I found them or they located me, I was ecstatic, and then bereft. For then there I was again at the same place I started, the beginning of a page or a voice. I garnered hope, but hope is wistful and empty and is like water in our hands.

I confess. At this moment in the time and context of being a writer in America, I don't know whether I believe or know anything that I once thought I believed or knew about our art of truth-telling, of singing, of constructing the next world as a story or series of stories that we will eventually inhabit, as will our children and their children. Maybe we've all been through this before, but it's another version and we're in it deep. I used to imagine writing as a ladder leading us from the blind world into the knowing world, but now to imagine a ladder means to imagine a land or a house on which to secure a ladder. For many of us in these lands now called America, imagining this place has been a tricky feat, because there is no place that hasn't or won't get stolen, polluted, or destroyed, and for all of us now planted here, the foundation is shaky, because though it is strong with vision, the country was founded on violent theft. But this is what we have, who we are, here, together. And we can use the fire still burning there to destroy this place, or build it anew with bricks made of the trash, with fresh, shining inspiration. The elm is still growing there in that yard.

Maybe the ultimate purpose of literature is to humble us to our knees, to that know-nothing place. Maybe we here on this planet are a story gone awry, with the Great Storyteller frantically trying out different endings. Whatever the outcome, we need new songs, new stories, to accompany us wherever we are, wherever we go. That's the power contained in a book, journal, or magazine that you can carry in your hands. So, these stories, poems, and songs are offered as such, as gifts for challenge, for inspiration, for sustenance.

CHRIS ABANI

Fire

—*for Bei Dao*

Lost, but for the flames we drag
through dark streets; smoke and dust
Aho je la, aho je la, aho jengeje, aho jengeje
This chant is sky orotund with sun
and the mirage: a pot smoldering
against night's face, startling last year's
spirits gathering in corners, holding on.
And this— The crackle
of burning firewood, a train of palm fronds
like hungry tongues licking the street,
parched from the intensity. Distant,
beyond the brood of dark hills the sea;
salt and stone. This is not superstition.
This is how we write love.

A I

Sisterhood

For what it's worth,
once I left the convent,
but I never left the Church.
It's true, I left Ireland in a hurry, too.
You could say I broke the habit,
or to quote my da'
"I pulled a rabbit out o' my arse"
and realized I put the cart before the horse
and wasn't going anywhere,
certainly not to Heaven
with my sparse faith.
I'd come late to thinking
that when I beat my breasts three times
and said my prayers, no one was listening,
not even Father Patrick in confession,
who did his own magic trick
of pulling forgiveness out of thin air
for you can do all sorts of things
when nothing's there to stop you.
Everywhere I looked I saw the forms that evil took
and all of them were pleasing,
all bent on deceiving poor wretched Catholics
into believing that an Act of Contrition
and a few Hail Marys could save them
from the very things they craved,
so one day I says to Mother Superior, "I'm leaving."

On the ship to New York, I tossed my rosary overboard
sure and didn't it float upon the water
a full three minutes before it sank
and I felt nauseous and faint
and lay down and fell into a deep sleep
and dreamed of slaughtered sheep bleeding and bleating,

until I screamed myself awake.
Soon after I arrived in New York,
I bought another rosary
and kept it under my pillow and didn't dream at all,
maybe because it seemed as if my life was a dream.
Alone in the gloomy rooming house in Brooklyn
I made peace with myself
and stopped wondering how I would survive
my separation from Christ's side.
No longer His bride, no longer free to hide
behind His sanctity, I was beside myself,
until I joined a community of former priests and nuns.
I moved into their brownstone, having found a home at last
where I could pass for being just another Colleen
who'd dreamed of a better life in America.
I was only twenty-five in 1964, you see
and didn't know yet how cruel men could be,
but I learned soon enough
when I lost my virginity, or should I say, gave it away
to a scoundrel who left me pregnant.
By then I was a practical nurse.
I treated women left in the lurch by other scoundrels,
yet, I fell for one myself.
One day at work, I miscarried.
A week later, I called my da' and told him.
He only asked, "Was he Irish, lass?"
"He was black," I answered.
"Black Irish that's all right," he said.
"No, he was black American," I said, "you know, Negro."
"You mean you did it with a Blackamore?" he shouted
and hung up.
Soon after that, the scoundrel came 'round again.
He brought me roses
and got on his knees and proposed.
I was frozen to the spot.
I could not speak, but finally just laughed
as defensively, he said
he wanted to make an honest woman of me.
I said God had already tried

and look what happened.
I'd hurt his pride, I know, but so what, I thought.
I'd lost my child
and anyway, what kind of father would he be?
He was perpetually broke,
and a stranger to responsibility,
admittedly to be expected because he was a fiddler
in an Irish band. "What's the black fellow doing here?"
people would ask and if he overheard them,
he would say, "I'm Creole from New Orleans."
He was a handsome devil indeed
who didn't need a wife.
"What you need," I told him, "is me out of your life,
so I'll take my chances with dishonesty."

After a year, I decided to move west.
I tried San Francisco, L.A., and finally Las Vegas on a whim
where one night when I was two sheets to the wind
I put a quarter in a slot machine
and to the accompaniment of ringing bells,
coins poured from its orifice into my hands.
They comped me for the night
and wouldn't you know
that in a penthouse high above the desert
I found my God again
with an Elvis record playing on the stereo
and in the very bosom of sin
where I lay my head that morning
when at last I fell asleep?
That afternoon, as I sat alone, the telephone rang
and I received a call to join a gentleman
who'd seen me the night before.
"I'm not a whore," I said, then instantly regretted it.
After apologies on both sides,
I decided to accept the invitation.
Anyway, it was only the other side of the casino
where the permanent residents, or denizens stayed.
At last, I was led into a room
and to my astonishment, the man standing

with his back to me turned suddenly
and instantly, I knew who he was.
"Ma'am," he said, in that faintly Southern accent
I'd heard only the night before
and here he was in person,
overweight and wearing a snakeskin jumpsuit,
snakeskin cowboy boots, and enough jewelry
to open a store.
He bade me take a seat on the white leather couch
and I sank deep into it as if it were fabric.
"Gotcha," he said. "Soft, ain't it."
I agreed, trying to keep my amazement at bay.
"I watched you play," he said. "You're lucky,
I can tell. Can't I?" he asked the guy
who'd brought me. He nodded yes
and while they waited expectantly
I only said, "Not really."
"Honey," said Elvis, "I'm never wrong.
Ask the Colonel."
At that I noticed a man standing back in the shadows
of the room. He came forward then
and stared at me as if demanding that I agree
and I did finally.
"Now," said Elvis, "let's eat."
And so we did. Late lunch, I guess you'd call it
a distressing amount of food appeared as if by magic
and he ate so much I feared he would explode,
but no, after a self-satisfied belch and a wink
he said, "I think I'll take a nap.
Feel free to stick around and hey, take something
as a souvenir, something that says the King, you hear?"
"I was a nun," I blurted.
And he said, "Hon, I knew there was something about you.
You were playing with Jesus."
I only smiled. I didn't know what else to do
and after a while, I left.

As I walked through the casino,
I knew I was going home.

When I set foot on the aul sod
I didn't feel like kissing it.
I hadn't missed it. Much.
I tasted the salt in the air
then I savored the faint, sweet flavor of melancholy,
but when I realized I was back for good
next thing I knew, I was in a pew,
praying my heart out,
praying I had enough strength to undo the past,
but the past cannot be undone,
only lived through.
I remembered watching the blood flow down my legs
and begging Jesus to save my sweet baby,
but also thinking it was my punishment
for leaving the Church.
How could I go back now, I thought,
as I sat daydreaming
about an existence full of meaning
I'd imagined being a nun would give me.
Had I been too young to understand
that self-sacrifice was part of the plan
had I let myself be enticed by the world,
then abandoned by it, or to it?
I couldn't tell.
My life was like a tightly woven black cloth
I couldn't see through, but could feel its weight
upon my body as I kneeled down,
praying to the Blessed Virgin
who stood beneath the Cross when she lost her Son.
Had the awful wound of his death ever left her thoughts,
had I returned to bear witness to my own poor truth.
Oh, reckless youth, I murmured,
covering my face with my hands
when suddenly, I heard a baby crying.
At first, I thought its mother would quiet it,
but the crying continued and finally,
I went to see what could be done,
but I couldn't see anyone.
"Hello," I called, but receiving no response,

I started to search the pews
which led me to a corner near the confessional
where I found a baby,
dressed in a christening gown.
I tried to soothe her by cooing like the doves
who lived above my room at the convent
and soon, she quieted.
When I took her to the priest,
he said, "A foundling,"
but I said, "A miracle."
He disagreed and said, "A sin."
Then looking hard at me, he said,
"She's your daughter, isn't she?"
I answered, "Yes, I was only trying
to do what was best for her."
He said, "But you're not a girl.
You know that life is full of disappointment and strife.
You have to rise above your troubles.
We'll pray for guidance."
"But Father," I protested gently, "it's time for her to eat."
And so I made my escape to motherhood,
or was it a retreat?
Then I knew what I would do,
although I did not know how I would manage.
You could say I took her in, or rescued her
or maybe she rescued me.
When I went to see my da',
cradling the baby in my arms,
he asked, "Is this the black one?"
"That was long ago. It died, remember?"
He said no, he was getting old,
but anyway, this one didn't look black at all.
"Are you back to stay?" he asked.
I said, "I am.
Is that all right?"
"I wouldn't mind the company," he said,
including the baby with a nod of his head.
"What's her name?" he asked.
I told him, "Faith."

Evolution

Loss and ruin grind under our feet
like spilled salt, bad luck sticking
to our soles. And joy
streaks across the sky, a star
burning out. Who knows
what will save us?

A man yanks the hair
of a woman he once covered with kisses.
Each kiss was a blossom and he thought
he was making his own garden.
All over the world there is failure.

Our species can enter the human
body with a laser, repair the shape
of a cornea to sharpen all it sees,
or crack the ribs, lift the heart
from its home, and plant it back again,
this exquisite intelligence—a brain
firing 100 billion neurons
(300 million in the octopus, 350 in the leech)—
is still bashing itself on the skull with big rocks.

All over, staggering
beauty, intricate and connected.
Under our skin are rivers and streams.
We can see them through the transparent cells.
And inside the modest and flamboyant organs
of plants a vegetal sex is taking place.
If you lie still in a soundproof room
you can hear the high tone
of your nervous system and the low
tone of your blood.

What kind of patience can we learn?
In caves the thinnest strands of stalactite extend
a centimeter in a hundred years, a single drop
of water hanging from each tip, returning
its burden of mineral to stone.

Goats chew the brilliantly
long green grass. Wind carries rain
across fields in dark transparencies.
It sings in the gutters, the earliest song on earth.
Lovers keep breaking each other open
like soft fruit, trying to bury their souls
in each other's flesh.
As termites undo the material world,
taking apart the day, still
the universe is expanding,
so precisely held in the web of tension
that we sleep at the edge of an ocean,
a child plays in the surf. We can pour
a cup of tea and stir sugar into it.

In Chad, with all that sand blowing, burying
the tents each night, biting skin, grit
everywhere, someone cradles the skull
of a being born seven million years ago.

O primitive brain, perhaps it's you
we should pray to, heaping our altars
with spliced DNA and the score to Bach's *Magnificat*,
one hair from Mother Teresa, Gandhi's dhoti,
and a tin cup of clear water. We could bow
through the long night, prostrate,
breathing in and breathing out.

Building the Rock Wall

The heart of the builder
the wild talent, the so-called genius of the artist
is largely overrated.

He has been building walls for 60 years now.
Two things are important.

Endurance
(Strength is useful but overrated;
leverage can accomplish at least as much as
the imprecision of brute force),

and *material,*
the second thing,
even more important.

Discard the crooked stones,
choose only the squarest,
sturdiest, finest ones.
The subject is everything.

In the presence of great stone,
the mason matters almost not at all,
needs only to be present each day.

Will

To the locusts that blur the tiny lyres of their shells,
I leave my blindness at the end of day.
To the distant whistle of the train at dusk,
I leave the smoke in a girl's hair.
To days I dipped my body in, I leave my only shadow.

To the gravel road that crackles like a tree on fire,
to the fluster of the wheel, the brake,
the broken shoulder, its buckle and curve,
to the long labor of the open eye,
I leave one lush confession.

To the pincers of ants dismantling a bird,
I leave the bitter patch at the tip of my tongue.
To the porch light haloed in a scribble
of moths, I leave my boyish appetite.
To the hymn, the yawn, the three in the morning,

I leave the warmth of the engine
as it settles and purrs.
To the empty page beneath me where I lie,
I leave the weight of black above.
To the hole that is my throat, I leave the flesh around it.

To the dream I can't remember,
I leave the one I won't. To my father's memory,
I leave the bread crumbs of my name.
To the body that follows a body to its grave,
I leave the seagull's laughter.

To the bride who says goodbye to the mirror,
I leave the other side of the mirror.
To the one who reads, I leave the room.
To the quiet deepening behind me as I go,
I leave the quiet to come.

MELANIE CESSPOOCH

Traveling Through Arizona

I left my house of silence and wrecked my body on the beach
    of travel.
An ocean of bus lines, planes with twin engines, and rubber
    balls that tumble down stairwells.
The road chooses women with shopping bags and greasy
    faces.
It pushes them toward the distance of gas stations and beer
    stands.
Because she looks like me in 40 years time, I stop and wait for
    her heavy body to fill the passenger seat. She half smiles
    under the hair that swishes in front of her eyes.
She doesn't have socks on and the coffee stains dribbled on
    her chest have taken her from tending sheep, washing
    dishes, and rinsing clothes.
She said her boyfriend left her stranded; an abandoned old
    ship, house, and car sit between us.
She said he was looking for his ex-wife.
I have nothing to offer.
The sandwich I bought to settle the knot in her chest was
    bitten and wrapped up.
I gave her ten dollars and my home address where she could
    send a payback, a gift, a note of survival.
She invited me to party out in the still desert; I told her I was
    traveling and the sun was not going to wait.
The house would not stay warm.
The water was too salty.

Study Hall, Deterritorialized

The brown boy hits me, but says he is sorry. The brown girl, his sister, says it's because he likes me. I say, *Yuk! He likes me? Well, I hate him.* The black girl pinches me and says, *Scaredy-cat, tattle-tale, little pussy...I dare you to hit back.* The white girl grabs my Hello Kitty purse and spills my milk money. I karate-chop her arm. The white boy says, *My father says that your father's egg rolls are made of fried rat penises.* I answer, *Yep, my father says that the reason why his egg rolls are made of fried rat penises is because white people are stupid idiots and like to eat fried rat penises.* The black girl laughs deep from her gut and high fives me. Just as I am redrawing the map, my little fresh-off-the-boat cousin from Malaysia starts weeping into her pink shawl like a baby, *Wa wa wa.* The white girl muffles her ears: *Can't you shut her up?*

I say, *Don't cry, little cousin, it's not as bad as it seems. It's verse!* I point to the window and magically, to entertain us, two fat pigeons appear cooing on the sill. The boy is sitting on top of the girl, trying to molest her. She is wobbling, shuffling, pirouetting under his weight...He is pecking a red bald spot on her skinny neck and singing:

> *We real cooooool   we real foooooools...*
> *We real cooooool   we real foooooools...*

Finally, we all laugh as one; laughing and laughing at God's beloved creatures. Behind this spectacle, against all odds, from the west, a strong explosion of sun bullies through the big- gray- loogie- of- a- cloud.

Winter, 1979

I squeezed the trigger, and another steel beer can wobbled off the fence post with the dull ping of a shiny copper BB. Cocking the gun again, I heard Monkey Tail and Cookie far off. Their sounds came at me slowly, in waves, like an echo. That meant Lonny was on his way. When you saw Lonny coming down the dirt road with his dogs and shotgun, you knew we'd arranged it at school the day before. For us, telephones were exotic, shining objects in other people's houses—exotic like aquariums, color TVs, or doorbells. Hell, the VCR was only a few years away, and still we drove twenty minutes to use the payphone in the booth at the corner of 12th and Broadway. Anyway, you really didn't *see* Lonny coming, you *heard* him, or rather his beagles and their aggressive nonstop yelp and yap. When I heard the clear jangling of chains, I knew—without looking—that Lonny was unlocking the swinging gate. I shot down one more can and stomped off through the frozen pasture to meet him.

The black-and-tan dogs trotted past me, snorting and whimpering at the ground, trailing their breath. I was over at Lonny's when his uncle gave him the two pups and Lonny acted like he'd just been given a stack of money. Now he walked up in his blaze orange vest and cap, smiling big, holding the .20 gauge broken open—across his arm—in textbook fashion. Lonny was nothing if not careful. That was the only reason my grandparents allowed me to hunt with Lonny and his gun. I wasn't conscientious; hence the BB gun.

"I heard you comin' a mile away," I told him.

"I ain't tryin' to be sneaky now," he said, and we shook hands—an elaborate ritual involving palms, fingers, snapping, clapping, and pointing. Red shotgun shells lined the front of his vest like teeth.

"I can smell me some rabbit fryin' already," he said, licking his lips and patting his stomach. He made his eyes get real big. I laughed like always. It was good to be out hunting and not worrying about catching the bus to school the next morning. It was Christmas vacation.

We began to follow the dogs, taking it easy, feet crunching snow. There would be nothing here, around the house. Our object was the open field ahead, past the pond. Although snow covered pasture everywhere, tips of brown grass showed on little mounds here and there, and blackberry bushes were beginning to expose their skeletons. Clouds were breaking after rows of sunless and snowy days, and when sunlight hit momentarily, the snow gleamed like sugar and we had to squint our eyes.

We plodded past my little white house. It looked so quiet and peaceful. Woodsmoke rose from it in a straight thin line, and the windows were steamed around the corners. A tumbling stack of firewood sat on the front porch, covered with a sky-blue tarp. I took the cookie Lonny offered me and bit off half of it. Chocolate. Ahead, Monkey Tail froze at a clump of brush and dug at it with his front legs, barking. Snow, then dark black dirt sprayed out in an arc.

Lonny laughed. "He still ain't nothin' but a pup," he said, cradling the gun against his shoulder like a soldier.

When we went hunting, I followed Lonny. He was a hunter, knew where to look, how to field-dress, look for sign. The extent of my hunting prior to Lonny had been with a long-ago cousin, blasting squirrels out of their nests with a .410. It was a roulette shot from underneath, and if one was home it flew out and plopped heavy and lifeless a few feet away. But when we went fishing, I was the leader. At first, Lonny didn't even know how to throw his line in. I taught him and even gave him my old Zebco 33 rod-and-reel. The pond where we fished at most was just ahead, powdered with snow, a squatting oval rink.

I knelt and refilled my gun by putting the BBs in my mouth and spitting them rapid-fire into the little hole in the barrel. I'd seen my cousin do that. It left an oily taste but was worth it since it sounded cool. When full the gun didn't rattle and felt hefty and solid—more like a real gun. I looked out over the field. All white. Cows massed together like statues next to the tree line, and beyond that, red lights of the three AM radio towers blinked steadily, like a pulse, glaring now in the dim light. As I stood, both dogs raised their usual yelping and howling to demonic levels. We had a German shepherd who had just recently disappeared and he barked, but nothing like this. I listened in amazement, but Lonny was already tugging my arm.

"C'moan," he said. "They on, they on."

We took off at a light jog. Only in the Arctic does a rabbit blend in with the snow. Around here they were gray with little white cottontails you couldn't help but keep your eyes on as they scooted and bounded, hugging the ground with electric velocity. The rabbit dashed out to a good lead, then slowed to suck the dogs in. At the last possible instant, with the dogs literally at his tail, it slashed a hard immediate left, ears flattened. As pure a ninety-degree angle as nature will allow. When Monkey Tail fell down rolling, trying to copy the turn, I heard a grumple in his throat. Cookie stayed on her feet but swung way out wide—totally out of the race, it seemed. But Monkey Tail wiggled off his back, and Cookie recovered by pivoting her rear like a bull turning to charge, and quickly they were in chase again. Always there was the constant, maddening bark-howl, which seemed to fill the universe. Lonny held up a hand, and we stopped and knelt by a blackberry bush. The trio was rounding the north bank of the pond like it was a racetrack. Monkey Tail and Cookie were side-by-side, the lead changing only when one or the other fell for a trick the rabbit pulled. The rabbit came at us in a jittery gray blur.

"They're running him right at us," Lonny said, and I saw the pride in his eyes. Without looking he jammed three shells into the gun. "This one's dead meat."

When Lonny rose and aimed, the rabbit veered left and ran straight across the pond. Lonny lifted the barrel momentarily, then leveled and shot and missed, and when he pumped, a red shell popped out at my feet. He shot again and missed, kicking up snow right behind the rabbit's feet, and on the third shot the rabbit cartwheeled and spun around and around like a disc in the middle of the pond. I jumped and yelled, high-fiving.

Bluish smoke seeped from the gun, the shots rang away in waves. The beagles chased after the rabbit and went silent when they hit the surface, sprawling like one of those baby deer in the Disney cartoons. Pink tongues hanging and breath steaming into the air, they stood over the rabbit.

Lonny whistled at them, and they raised their heads but would not move. They lowered and shook their heads like cattle and whimpered. We jogged up to the edge of the pond, and Lonny called again, whistling, but they would not come.

"Dang it," Lonny said.

Lonny tested the ice with a foot and then walked out while I circled and tried to call the dogs. They wouldn't listen to me. As Lonny neared they waggled their rumps and Lonny began to talk to them and they barked again and everything seemed normal until I heard a wicked *crack!* and a long split struck out like lightning and Lonny plunged in over his head. He bobbed up screaming and frantically grabbed at the edge of the hole and was half-out when a big jagged plate broke off and he went under again on his back. I ran around the bank to where I was closer to him and stepped out onto where the ice was thick, then I got on my stomach and inched toward him. I screamed his name. He was able to turn around in the water and grabbed at my BB gun. He got one hand around the barrel, then the other, and I pulled and pulled and finally he was able to get a leg up onto the ice and crawl out.

We banged into the house. Granny was at the kitchen table, stringing together acorn shells we would use to decorate the tree Grandpa Chester had cut down. Curling red strips of tin—cut from Grandpa's Prince Albert cans—were strewn about the table.

"Oh my word, what on earth?" Granny said.

I told them what happened in a rush of run-on sentences and gestures while Lonny stood shivering, hugging himself with a vacant stare. Running to the house, the water had frozen on his jeans and in his hair. We led him to the front room and stood him beside the King woodstove glowing red at the sides. It made a steady sucking sound, like wind. We held our hands over it and rubbed them together.

Grandpa sat in his chair in the corner holding the newspaper out in front of him. When he was reading the paper or watching a football game on TV, you invariably had to repeat yourself when you talked to him. He sat there reading as we shivered and hopped next to the woodstove.

Finally he said, "You boys shoot anything? Where's all them rabbits?"

"Lonny fell in the ice and lost his dogs and gun and everything." I was looking at and talking to the front page of the newspaper.

"Huh?" he said, preoccupied, still moving his head over the columns.

I repeated what I'd said.

Slowly, he eased down the paper, revealing his white hair and magnified eyes behind the rubber-banded reading glasses.

"Whaaat?" he said, drawing it out. He looked at Lonny in wonder, took in the soaked clothes. It seemed to hit him all at once. "Well, son of a buck."

Granny led Lonny to the hot bath she had run and told me to dig up some clothes for Lonny to wear and for me to towel off and put on warm clothes.

When Lonny was in the bathroom my uncle said, "What's the little coon crying about?"

Growing up one of us was always staying with Granny. In this way I was always meeting one great-uncle or the other. But this one—Elliott—was new to me. He'd showed up the day before, huge, literally filling the doorway, holding a Christmas present for Granny in one hand and a bottle of whiskey in the other. These uncles were always showing up out of nowhere. You looked for a car or something out next to the truck, but there wasn't anything.

I hung up the sheet to block them out and took off my clothes and toweled off. I felt bad for Lonny, like crying, too. Everything happened so fast. One second we were joking around, watching the dogs chase the rabbit, and the next second Lonny was bobbing in the ice water and the pups were sinking. They went under without ever making a sound. I knew Lonny was crying over the dogs and not the shotgun. I heard him splashing around in the bathwater. I put warm clothes on and went back to the woodstove.

Elliott came into the room. He had short hair and tennis shoes—unlike my other uncles, most of whom had long hair and wore cowboy-type clothes.

"Hey, old sport," he said, then tried to give me the old one-two, acting like he was boxing me. He had whiskey breath. I liked him okay but right then didn't feel like boxing around with him and having him jab me on the arm and scruffing my head. The night before he'd showed us some pictures of rodeos. He was wearing a Gilligan's cap and fake toothy smile. He had on cutoff blue jean shorts over red tights and a pair of high-top Converse. The picture said "All-Indian Rodeo, Barona, California, 1978." It was taken from above, and Elliott was looking up into the camera. Last night he told me I'd never make it as a bulldogger if I didn't toughen up. Then came the boxing lessons and the wrestling, which only tickled and made me breathless.

"Lonny just fell into the pond," I said. "His dogs went under, too."

"You ever been to California?" he said.

"No," I said, watching the ash breathe red and gray underneath the vent. There was a tin box under the vent to catch stray chunks of coal and ash.

Elliott pointed westward, shook his head, and frowned. I didn't understand him at all. He drank from his bottle again and staggered back into the kitchen.

Granny was letting the car warm up. Lonny and I sat in back, and Elliott was with Granny in the front. Lonny had on a pair of my sweats, a sweater, and a jean jacket and cap we'd found in the closet. He'd begun to loosen up. Maybe the shock was wearing off, but I could tell he was still troubled. Elliott reached around and grabbed Lonny by the throat and said real slowly, gritting his teeth, "You fucking nigger."

Everything froze. Snow drifted lazily in the air outside the car, big flakes which floated and twirled silently, silently. Lonny gripped the armrest, eyes wide in alarm. Elliott's dark bangs curved over and partially obscured his eyes. His teeth showed. There was a big turquoise ring around one of the fingers around Lonny's neck.

"Here now, Elliott," Granny said, "that's Jordan's friend. Let him be. Everything's okay."

Elliott held his position. The little car rumbled. Steam rolled up into the air from the rear. It was beginning to warm up. The fingers came off Lonny's neck one by one. Elliott turned up a bottle and finished the clear liquid in three big gulps. He rolled down the window and flung it into the snow. He laughed.

"Oh, hell. He knows I'd never hurt him," he said.

You fucking nigger.

All this was years and years ago; yet those three words stuck with me. It wasn't like it was the first time I'd heard the word. But it was the only time I'd heard it said with venom. Until then it was only a word. A word like grasshopper, baseball, flower, or rain. I heard it all the time. Those were the days of afros, picks, and bell-bottoms. The school bus I rode home on with Lonny was all black except for me and the driver. *Nigger, this; nigger, that; nigger, hell; nigger, please.* Mine was the last stop. The district wouldn't allow the bus down the dirt road. The driver turned around at the end of the pavement in The Village—as my grandparents nicknamed the all-black neighborhood. It wasn't like housing projects or anything. These were houses the blacks themselves built in the twenties or thirties. Squat little wood houses with green shingling and various pens and hutches nearby for slaughter stock.

By the time I got on the bus it had already picked up Muskogee High and Alice Robertson Junior High. Usually, I had to stand. Always, I was the last one off unless Lonny walked home with me to fish until it grew dark. The day before Lonny and I went hunting, I rode in back with him singing "I Wish." Lonny and his partner hammered out the beat with their hands against the seats. Usually I didn't join in, but that day I'd caved in and sang along. I saw Lonny nudge a friend with his elbow and nod toward me, laughing. The whole bus was like a carnival every afternoon: hellish loud laughing, fighting, arguing, shouting. My ears rang after I'd departed. One afternoon the driver—a kindly old white-haired man with roundish eyeglasses—stopped the bus and said in a very pleasant voice, looking at us in the mirror, "Now, boys and girls, we'll have to keep the noise down." I thought, *We aren't boys and girls, we're niggers.* I'm sure I was the only person on the bus who even heard him, anyway.

Growing up, nigger was quite the common term. I never heard Granny use it—she always gave people the last possible benefit of the doubt—but Chester used it on occasion. Meadowlark were nigger quail. A carp or gar was nigger fish.

For football at lunchtime recess it was blacks, Indians, and Filipinos versus the whites. Which meant the blacks, me, and James Suero from Manila, whose dad was a doctor at nearby Muskogee General. One day we were to pick up James for a baseball game because his parents were out of town. They lived in a fancy addition near Pershing School. Sweeping driveway, lawn like a golf course, bay windows, doorbell. I rang it. The chimes cascaded. A black woman answered wearing a business-like navy blue skirt and a white cap of some sort. I stammered that I was looking for James Suero. She invited me in. On the way to the truck I asked who the woman was.

"Oh, that's my mom," James Suero said.

When Suero saw my face, he laughed.

"Aw, man, that's our maid, you turkey."

I felt embarrassed for the woman. I didn't know anyone had maids anymore.

Lonny and I played another season of ball the next summer, which was cut short for him when a fiddleback bit him near the armpit after he'd put on a T-shirt which had been lying on the floor all night. It rotted out his flesh and took all season to heal, leaving an angry red scar. Still, he came to games and practices wearing his white sling. He didn't quit the team. We wound up going to different junior highs in town, and Lonny quit playing baseball, while I continued. We saw each other ever so often during high school, but I heard that he quit and began attending vocational school for air conditioning.

Then, several years later after I graduated college in California, I returned to Muskogee and to the little junior college there to check on a transcript. I was walking across the parking lot, and there sat Lonny in an old blue truck with hutches in back. Our eyes met, and he gave that silent, teethy laugh of his, bobbing his head. He got out of the truck, and we shook hands—not the same ritual we went through as kids but close to it. Waiting on his girlfriend to get out of class, he was drinking tall-boy beers in cans and offered me one. It was a summer evening, and the sky was milky blue, lit up from underneath. It was warm, and stars were beginning to appear. The beer was cool and sweet.

Lonny looked the same, only a little chubbier. He had a thicker Southern accent than I'd remembered, or possibly it was because I had been in California four years. I told him what I'd been doing. His eyes sparkled. I remembered he'd been a brother to me growing up. He told me he worked at Madewell Metals, recycling scrap iron and aluminum. We remembered the time we were making fun of Chester because he pronounced it "alumy-num," which, frankly, is what it looks like on paper if you think about it.

Granny sat us down and told us not to make fun of Chester. He never got to finish school, she said. He had to go to work in the fields when he was only twelve years old and he still works hard every day to feed me, she said.

We were leaning against the tailgate, being secretive with the beer. Inside the bed of the truck lay fishing rods and empty beer cans. It was then I noticed the two beagle pups in the hutches. Lonny got them out and held one up, and it licked his face. Lonny grimaced but let the dog lick his face. One of the dogs barked, and all the memories came swimming over me. The Christmases with the real trees Chester would cut down when we went riding around on scouting expeditions in the country, my uncle Elliott, the youthful lifetime of so-so baseball teams.

"Hold up your arm, Lonny," I said. "Let me see your scar."

Lonny put his beer down and raised his arm. I traced my fingers over it. There were raised purple welts where flesh used to be.

"You remember that," Lonny said evenly.

I nodded and finished my beer. Lonny's girlfriend came out of one of the nearby brown buildings. Lonny introduced us. She was a pretty girl, but shy behind her thick glasses. I told Lonny the usual: that I'd call, I'd write, or I'd drop by. He still lives in the same house, and one of these days I actually might do it.

SANDRA CISNEROS

In My Little Museum of Erotica

In my little museum
of erotica
I would place your feet.

I would place your feet
sandwiching
my feet.

Their softness.
Their heat.

And I would
place your arms
as you do mornings,
beneath my neck.
around my waist,
tugging me towards you,
my back to your chest.

This
well-beingness
I would set
on a Corinthian
column.

And those
who are aesthetes
of mornings and feet
would say, Ah!
Yes!

JAN CLAUSEN

Instead of an Epithalamion

Well we did our best in deracinated weather.
Daughters were wedding daughters, suddenly.
They'd registered at Bed Bath & Beyond.
Rain-hurled catalpa flowers bruised the yard.
The dual-mothered bride procured a dress,
to her surprise. Pert cannabis jungled up.
One wandered under oaks, umbrella'd to the hilt,
like some female in a lyric or a play,
the sort who'd *labor to be beautiful,*
forsooth. (That poet didn't do the math.)
Once mothers bedded down and chivvied death
(the "Great Behind"); now rivers hurry home
while marriage gathers its divorce-bouquet:
a shivaree of artless exes in the fray.

Ghost Deer

There are deer here.
I can feel them.
Antler firm, pelt soft
lingering close-by.

Ghost deer.
Albino white.
The entire herd
a miracle.

Wondrous revelations
occur rarely,
once a lifetime.
Here, twenty-four

Snuggle treelines
wintertime
camouflaged.
Sisters of mine.

Cold Reading

It's really cold in here now,
easily forty below something,
and half the class is asleep.

Snow dazzles in the windows,
makes a cake of each desk.
It's really cold in here now.

I've been lecturing on the same
poem for twenty-six hours
and half the class is asleep.

I want them to get it. I start
to talk about death again
and it's really cold in here now.

One student has frozen solid,
her hair snapping off in the wind
and half the class is asleep.

"See that," I say, "Lisa gets it."
But it's so cold in here now
half the class are white dunes
shifting to the sea.

JON DAVIS

A Choir of Misprisions

Gone, the quiet of toads.

We used to see them half-burrowed in the powdery dirt.

I liked their eyes, the nictating membrane.

They seemed wry, a little smug.

Like a girl who is double-jointed.

Demonstrating that.

At recess.

Gone the articles, how they coddled their nouns.

Or, sometimes, volunteered them.

Did I mention the car crash?

That gone, too.

Did I mention the lost reveries of childhood?

A career, you say?

Built on those?

How strange.

Must have been a slight career.

There was a bittern in a white pine.

I got so close.

Held an owl on my finger under a sky of crows.

The subtext kept leaching into the text.

In therapy, they would call it "Fear of Abandonment."

You could almost hear the capital letters.

There should have been a twelve-step program for the cats, hissing and swatting each other on the lawn:

> *I mated with your mother.*

> *I ate the mouse you were toying with (and which you were probably saving for dinner).*

> *I lapped up the milk your owner intended for you.*

> *I acknowledged a higher power, but there seemed to be a mechanism somewhere inside and—bad news—it wasn't a brain.*

The good news—I read it this morning—is that the male mantis gets to keep his head.

I mean that literally.

Would that we were so lucky.

I mean that figuratively.

A career, you say?

The female mantises in the experiments were probably just hungry, underfed.

And the head is an excellent snack.

Except that the eyes and mouth are attached, one can imagine a
     cat getting through his day without one.

A horse, however, is a different story.

Not that there's much of importance there—just the source of a
     horse's errors.

Like mistaking the wind for a predator or mistaking the glint off a
     shard of glass for a predator or mistaking a cedar tree for
     a predator or mistaking a rubber ball for a predator or
     mistaking a predator for a barn door.

And what is a horse but a choir of misprisions.

Isn't that why we love to guide them?

Isn't that why they need us so?

But I was talking about childhood.

Lost reveries. "Fear of Abandonment."

Listen, you can almost hear the car starting, the clutch pedal's
     thump, the heart beating its fists inside the four-year-old's
     chest.

The Day Unwinds Like a Spool of Film

Moments connect like iron filings on a magnet,
Not by the clock moving forward
But by likenesses of mood; the way the sun
Strikes a plate glass window
At dawn unites all such dawns, the way love
Brightens the face of your lover after
Even the briefest absence, the same
Knotty dilemma, whether day or night,
Yesterday or today, leaves you running on a
Treadmill to nowhere. All sunsets
Are the same, all rain; the day is a deck
Of cards being dealt from the bottom.
How do you know each time we blink
We open our eyes to the same world? Heraclitus
Tells us the mind glues each moment
To the next by force of will. It could
All fall apart.

Alibi

I was waiting like a saint before the era of saints
as she searched the racks for just the right threads.
I was wondering after a hundred years,
which is the body and which the clothes,
although I would never ask her this.
I was staring at the girls behind the window
when she emerged in a purple robe,
the same old garb in which she arrived.
I was practically grown by then,
almost a giant with the Nimrod nose.
It was raining like never before
and we were in it the whole damn time,
floating in a sea above the mall.
How did she look when she went under?
Where were you when I called your name?

Anniversary Letter from Metropolis

Mon petit chou,
> no more great vows are said.
Can't save, extinguish, master, or attain—
My gusto blown to bits.
The carpenter shaves a door, below his breath

Sings *I got daisies in green pastures,*
I got my girl, who could ask for anything more?
The gutters overflow and eat concrete.
From upper decks, they blow their paper leaves

At crowds, stiff men in waistcoats. Dumbwaiters.
Rooftop pigeons' poppet heads tucked under wings:
From this low point, the graves are dizzying.
Mercutio,
> my hero, a rook who stirs up dust—

Don't move, don't be too bold.
Just be content to be the average Joe who sprints
Past FedEx, UPS, anything standing too long in the road,
Anyone who opens from the back.

The Poet's Coat

for Jeff Male (1946–2003)

When I cough, people duck away,
afraid of the coal miner's disease,
the imagined eruption of blood
down the chin. In the emergency room
the doctor gestures at the X-ray
where the lung crumples like a tossed poem.

You heard me cough, slipped off your coat
and draped it with ceremony across my shoulders,
so I became the king of rain and wind.
Keep it, you said. *You are my teacher.*
I kept it, a trench coat with its own film noir detective swagger.

The war in Viet Nam snaked rivers of burning sampans
through your brain, but still your hands
filled with poems gleaming like fish.
The highways of Virginia sent Confederate ghost-patrols
to hang you in dreams, a Black man with too many books,
but still you tugged the collar of your coat around my neck.

Now you are dead, your heart throbbing too fast
for the doctors at the veterans' hospital to keep the beat,
their pill bottles rattling, maracas in a mambo for the doomed.
On the night of your memorial service in Boston,
I wore your coat in a storm along the Florida shoreline.
The wind stung my face with sand, and with every slap
I remembered your ashes; with every salvo of arrows
in the rain your coat became the armor of a samurai.
On the beach I found the skeleton of a blowfish,
his spikes and leopard skin eaten away by the conqueror salt.
Your coat banished the conqueror back into the sea.

Soon your ashes fly to the veterans' cemetery at Arlington,
where once a Confederate general
would have counted you among his mules and pigs.
This poet's coat is your last poem.
I want to write a poem like this coat,
with buttons and pockets and green cloth,
a poem useful as a coat to a coughing man.
Teach me.

Paradise

I. *The garden of Eden. Also called* earthly p., *to distinguish it
    from* the heavenly p.

First

She is seventeen, he twenty-one.
She is a green girl, Ophelic but believing
Herself a witch-queen, while he plays Edmund,
Bastard and natural. Sitting on the cliff's edge, her
Back to the village where floats down the sound
Of wild clog-dancing and the cars of old women
Driving their drunk men methodically home,
She thinks, *I want to be like everybody else,
To hurt and love: I want to be human.*
Cue him: in the darkened theater a wisp of hair
Tickles her ear like a whisper and she is
Enchanted. Steal her right off if you can.

II. *Heaven, the abode of God and his angels and the final abode
    of the righteous. (Now chiefly* poet.*)*

Moonlight with its beautiful scatter of white lies...
On the hill we pass among wrought-iron crosses
Where people died in roadside accidents: you explain
Just as I decide to commit my own for ever.
Waving fields of hay as if for the yearly sacrifice—
The goddess is shaken and rises distraught,
She is not what she was. It is freezing in this dark
House put together like a coffin not meant to last
To the Resurrection: when we shall recover all
We have lost, sea-beasts spitting up their swallowed
Arms and legs and voices...

What is that noise?

My unhappiness.

What is that noise again that noise—
My unhappiness unfolding even unto heaven.

III. *A place like Paradise; a region of surpassing beauty, or of*
   supreme bliss.

Sure, come, you say, *for maybe, two days?* I
Don't understand yet but I will...in lovely Oslo,
The hair of people are full of light, their skin, their eyes
And it is the White Nights so even when we walk
Home near midnight the world is luminous.
I think I could stay this girl forever, a record
Spinning around in this kitchen singing you
This song; I'd watch you slowly change as the sun
Watches a tree grow or a balloon regards the little
Giggling boy who lets it go...an inch-length Buddha
Is trapped behind glass at the Viking Museum;
But how did it *get* here? *I don't know,* you grin.

IV. *An oriental park or pleasure-ground, esp. one enclosing wild*
   beasts for the chase.

Now let the universe explode

now let the ship of nails
Sail in, now Balder has received his death-blow
From the "harmless" mistletoe: see, he dared them try
To hurt his impermeable body but the trickster
With the gilded tongue found out where he was weak.
My mouth fills with rage like a cave with a thousand bats
Shitting their magnificent guano—but all too late,
For now in the dozen frozen attitudes of naïve agony
The fawns in the forest of my heart find they are
Shot down and turned to stone like these statues
In Vigeland's Park where it has just begun to rain
And I stand motionless in the pose of loneliness.

V. *A pleasure-garden; spec. the garden of a convent.*

Here in my cloister, I have you. In the city
Of ladies, in the courtyard of language
I immemorialize you. How does it feel to be
A god? Nero said *sweet, sweet, sweet as honey.*
I place your name sparingly on my tongue
As the Eucharist, and I don't share it
With anyone, making a new monica for you.
Finally one night I drink eleven clear stars, then
Open my mouth and vomit forth your story.
Little secret: you have your own holy books,
Pages of my diary, scriptures and interpretations
As if you were Kabbalah and I ordained.

VI. slang. *The gallery of a theater, where the "gods" are.*

From this distance you appear small, more like a puppet,
I can see where the joints of your mouth
Ride up and down, such a clumsy wooden nutcracker
I grow suspicious as to who's been on those ropes
All this time. Ten years gone—now I find you
Horribly shrunken, like a cannibal's prize skull
Down to the little chit you first were. So: it was *I*
Who blew you full of air, as a glassblower shapes her vase
Pinching the film into your expensive face. Thank you,
Thank you everyone; the part of the dead girl was played
By me, the part of the dog by the dog. Goodbye.

NOTES:
*Balder—Norse god, thought to be invincible until the trickster god Loki
    discovered his single weakness, mistletoe.*
*Ship of nails—in Ragnarök, the Norse end-of-days battle, a ship made of
    the fingernails of the dead will sail in, bearing the destroyers of the
    world.*
Vigeland's Park—sculpture garden in Oslo.

Playing House

We shelter best
that which destroys us. *Language.*

Speaking to the *other* is like this:

    standing on a small raft; baskets of apples to balance it;
    a murder of crows downstream.

There are no maps of the waters that cross through this house.
A shut door does no good.

Even pots with lids
will be smashed in the stream.

We each have tongues; each want to taste
the *insides,* the spillings of the other's winter stash.

If there was no house, there might be nothing
to displace. I have dreamt this ceiling of burrowing voices

so as to put them away into their own right place—
the impossible task of tidying a home.

It's not that we asked it in,
such a theater. The peripheries of the yard

had been protected *by the old ghosts,*
stuffing the last of our bread into holes in the hay

pecked out by habits of birds, *our own kind,*
who had always nested in the piñon.

They slipped in without knocking. A verb without a noun
does not *do* any *thing*. It's an invasion of swallows

thumping in the attic: displacement occurs
by the ones arriving *after*

the fact: we were each on our separate rooftops,
licking the sunset into our mouths, as if

it was not dying, as if
we each had the only roof.

If the shingles hadn't creaked beneath us,
we might never have had to speak about *it:*

fixed to a porch swing
so as to feel the crosswinds,

hollowed skin
like a tin mission,

our bones in the kitchen
fighting over the preserves. Once

the complete thought possessed nothing;
mud houses collapsed often in high tide;

wild weeds grew along this arroyo,
though they froze into spears in winter,

we walked gently among them,
unscathed by the light they captured.

Confession

Yes, I was utterly wrong,
I thought that humans were vertical wounds
against the horizon, feeding their own fissures
with wood and coal,
knocking constellations with empty heads,
smiling at desire with a missing golden tooth.
And they aren't like that,
instead, humans are just humans
like the songs that birds sing when
braiding with clouds the wind's hair.
Yes, I bred raving conjectures all these years.
I believed,
that stones were fossils,
that hands were flowers
and eyes, hungry wolves,
but, it is not like that,
stones are overlooked tears,
hands are smoked glasses,
eyes are roads that always lead to the sea.
Yes, I have never known much.
I thought that liquid meant solid
that three meant two and a half,
that You meant I.
And instead,
liquid is almost solid,
three means the infinite,
We are the Others not knowing that They are Us.

Fishing for Cats 1944

Sometimes we counted freight trains a hundred cars long,
carrying searchlights, wings, and fuselages to Montreal.

My grandfather and I found Luther's leaky old rowboat,
its oars shipped, across the railroad by Eagle Pond.

We pushed it into dark water, carrying sticks for poles
and the Bokar coffee can of worms I collected

digging with a spade in loam at the hayfield's edge.
We pinned the pink wriggly creatures onto small hooks

and he told me stories while we caught bony perch
to feed the barn cats at home. Only the old mother cat,

her teats hanging down to the barn floor, survived Chevys
and Model A's on Route 4, to breed more litters of kittens.

When I dug holes to bury the young ones, dead in the gutter,
I didn't care. For Sunday dinner we killed a setting hen

and laughed as she ran in circles with her head cut off.
In the *Boston Post* we read that the skies over Europe

were black all day with American boys bombing Germany.

Passover

The hotter the sun the whiter the bloom,
        my grandmother used to say of the dogwoods,
            Christ's trees, still bearing his blood,
and our hearts, of course,
                        in need of redemption.

On her cue, I'd wield a bowl of potato peels
        out past the barn to the hog pen
        where they snout-rooted mud-slime
and anything I threw them,
                        squealing indescribable glee.

I've spent my lifetime thinking on sin,
        on the dark place a heart is
        and the mind trying its best to slant it
otherwise, two prongs
                        like a snake's strike.

I've spent my lifetime shuffled back and forth—
        in awe of the leaf-shape, the fungus-browned bark;
        seeing everything as moral, as indictment of self.
Which is it?
            the thing as itself? or the lesson it teaches?

I'm thirty-three now, the age of Jesus when he said,
        "It is finished." At night the crickets deem the universe
        a simple place of ease, a drift toward the next day's
brilliance of light.
            I wake and undo. I pray these little blasphemes.

Dream of the Revolution

Poland, 1920

In darkness they at last reach the bridge at B—, which the retreating Poles in their fury have dynamited. Undaunted, the division commander consults his maps by lamplight and gives the order: "We will wade across." Horses, creaking carts, tachankas— the long column streams down the bank and plunges headlong into the black, slow river, past the fallen bridge. See him there, the young reporter, before fame touched him, before his fall, as he once wished himself seen, among soldiers. "So beautiful," the commissar murmurs beside him, dipping his hand in the water as their wagon pushes through muck and soft reeds and settles heavily in the current.

They are halfway across when K suddenly appears beside the wagon, crouched atop his beautiful horse like a circus gypsy, singing; it is this same raw energy which inspired the young reporter to describe the Cossack in his first and so far only published dispatch for *Red Cavalryman,* this same force of spirit which has made K something of a favorite among the men; favorite and source of amusement. "Remind us again, hero, where you got your little pony? What was that poor Yid's name whose skull you split open?" Lies, K insists; the others are merely jealous of him and his newfound celebrity. "My father gave me this horse," the Cossack announces fiercely, as if daring anyone to argue. The young reporter keeps his mouth shut. It is better that way, he consoles himself. If the Cossack is a thief, let history deal with him.

The scouts return at daybreak. There is another village up ahead, just beyond the next hill: a handful of huts, derelict farms, a lonely, half-looted church, and, farther along, a squat square schoolhouse fronting a small cottage. Each floats in glaring sunlight in the young reporter's field glasses, and each building is as desolate as the country looming around it. Except the schoolhouse, he discovers. A red flag hangs limply from the little bell tower in front of it, and as the column approaches, a man emerges from the schoolhouse, waving his arms. "Comrades," he calls out in Russian. "Welcome, brothers. Welcome."

He is the village schoolmaster. It is his red flag dangling like a cravat from the bell tower. As the column continues past, he and the young reporter stand in the fretwork of shade beneath the bell tower, drinking water from a tin cup. "This is the fourth appointment I've had in five years," the schoolmaster confides, brushing the dust off his striped trousers. "The first three, as soon as my neighbors found out I was a Marxist, they sent me packing." He smiles faintly, and the young reporter smiles back. The water they share tastes of metal. "May I show you something?" the schoolmaster asks.

"Of course."

Together they cross the schoolyard.

"Actually it's a good thing you arrived when you did," the schoolmaster admits. "I think some of my older students were beginning to talk to their parents about me, which is how it always starts. First the students talk, then the parents talk. The next thing you know, people are poisoning your dog. Which was what happened in the last village. Very unpleasant."

Just then one of the junior officers stumbles from the schoolmaster's cottage with a portable phonograph cradled in his arms like a lamb. "What are you doing with that, brother?" asks the schoolmaster. Requisition, the soldier says. Inside the cottage they discover the others, officers and enlisted men alike, stripping the room to the baseboards; furniture, photographs, rugs, it is all being carried away.

"I'll make sure you are issued the proper receipts," the young reporter promises, blushing with shame. It is all he can do: as a noncombatant attached to the division, as a reporter, a writer of agitprop.

"Receipts?" says the schoolmaster.

"For your losses."

Later, in back of the cottage, in a little library crowded with shelves, the schoolmaster crouches to retrieve a book. Behind him, a single sun-struck window overlooks a garden, fields.

"Old friend," the schoolmaster murmurs.

It is the prophet himself, the young reporter sees, a nearly perfect early printing of Marx's *Das Kapital*, which the older man commences to recite, from memory, in his sonorous, slightly hoarse lecturer's voice—in the original German, no less. It is only when the others in the next room begin to kick holes in the walls that he stops, pulling a handkerchief from his pocket and wiping the sweat from his brow.

"Please, go on," the young reporter says.

He does. Outside, K's horse, turned loose to graze, has found its way in from the fields and discovered the schoolmaster's garden, around which a waist-high fence of wattle and chicken wire leans on crooked posts. Like a machine set in motion, the horse stretches its long, linen-colored neck over the wattle fence and, as the young reporter watches, begins to delicately eat the flowers off one of the rosebushes; the blood-red petals that spill from its mouth are like the petals slaves once scattered at the feet of emperors, kings.

By nightfall the schoolmaster is gone, sent back of the line where he will be safe, the commissar assures the young reporter. Safe from what, the commissar will not say. The young reporter finds him sitting alone in the empty schoolhouse, censoring letters. "Why are you so worried about him?" the commissar asks. "What do you care?"

"He's a Marxist."

"He is a dilettante," the commissar says dismissively. The flickering lamp casts gloomy shadows across the rows of tables and benches. Its light shines wetly on the knobs of the wooden coat pegs on the wall behind the desk, and on the commissar's crisply parted, oiled black hair. "A bourgeois dilettante, for that matter." The scratching pen pauses. "How's your next article progressing, by the way?"

From the plains far north of the village, intermittently, comes the faint thunder of artillery—another division clearing the way west to Warsaw.

"Slowly," the young reporter says. In fact he has written virtually nothing since that night they crossed the river; only notes, sketches. He has, for the moment, lost his bearings.

"Our men need encouragement," the commissar says. "You

must give them hope. It is your responsibility to give them hope." His expression softens. "You know, I'm something of an admirer of yours. I used to read *New Life* religiously. Your articles in particular."

"You're from Petrograd?" the young reporter asks.

"Yes."

They are both quiet a moment.

"I suppose," the commissar says finally, "it must be a bit of an adjustment for you. Your new role."

My new role, the young reporter thinks. As what exactly? As reporter? As propagandist? In fact he is expected by his editors at *Red Cavalrymen* to balance both duties, if such a balance is possible: he is to be both journalist and tender of hopes.

The commissar tilts back in his chair. He is, for all his boundless confidence, himself a young man still. "He speaks German, you know. Your Marxist. Quite fluently. One of our officers overheard him."

The young reporter says nothing at first. Then, "So did Marx, I believe."

"Is that a joke?"

"Only an observation."

To the north the heavy guns finally fall silent. The legs of the commissar's chair creak, the lamplight flickers on the letters spread across the table. It was only a week ago, the young reporter thinks, that the commissar trailed his hand in the river; now that same hand censors letters to wives, lovers. "Well," he says, sighing, "good night, comrade."

"Good night."

It is a mild, moonless summer evening. Fires flicker in the yards of the cottages spread along the road, and in the weedy lots between cottages, and in the withered, water-starved fields. Near one campfire a phonograph plays—the schoolmaster's phonograph, warbling under stars.

That night he dreams of Petrograd. It is winter. Across the black Neva, anchored into the cloudy, snow-dusted ice, stretch even lines of track, but there are no clattering trams out today. He is older, years older, and yet the city is as it was when he was twenty, before the revolution. In the flat upstairs, a rich, deeply resonant voice, muffled by lathe and plaster, is reciting a poem to thunderous music: *By the White Sea we cast our nets into the cold blue waters and found a wondrous wonder, a most confounding wonder. A boot. And in this boot we found a note laid there: "In my searches I have met with mishap, my most cherished dream did not come true."*

The murmur of a plane draws him to another window. A parade is passing; hundreds of marchers fill the street, carrying sagging banners, carrying signs. Leaflets flutter down over the marchers from the ashy sky like enormous snowflakes, but the plane dropping them is nowhere to be seen; there is only the low tractor-like drone of its engine. On the bobbing signs, framed in gold like the holy icons of older parades, is the broad black silhouette of a face. A single drum, somewhere deep in the crowd, beats like a heavy, slowing heartbeat.

Opening the window, he leans out across the icy sill to snatch one of the leaflets as it drifts by.

Comrades! We have watched friends, brothers, husbands and wives—even our own children—march silently to their deaths, soldiers all in our great, glorious struggle. Everything we ever cherished, we have given. It was history that demanded this terrible sacrifice, comrades, history we were serving. But rejoice! Now, at last, when we have nothing more to give, when we can go no further, it is history that is dying, and we may rest.

Somewhere among his papers, he knows, these very same lines are written. They are his own words, words he will return to after the last of the marchers has vanished and he is alone again. The leaflet is heavy in his hand; it is still damp from printing, he sees, and the ink that bleeds onto his fingertips is as black as the Neva. Someone has begun to knock on his front door, someone is calling his name. Over Petrograd, like a ghost, the droning plane circles and circles.

This evening, over tea, the division commander and commissar discuss the Party's policy of summarily executing political enemies, as it was established in the early, uncertain months of the revolution. As policy, it is a practice both men support—the commissar admittedly with some reservation, idealist that he is. Instead their argument balances upon when such methods are to be carried out. "As often as is useful," the division commander grunts, crunching the hard lump of sugar in his mouth.

"Yes, but useful to whom?" asks the commissar. "After all, we don't want to end up like the Jacobins, up to our stirrups in blood. We must be better than the French."

"Dialectics and smoke." The division commander rubs his eyes. "This is war, comrade commissar. In war one must follow orders, without debate. If I am ordered by my superiors to shoot some fellow—even if I personally have nothing against this man—then I will shoot him without hesitation."

"And his wife? His children?"

"Yes. And you, too, comrade," the division commander says gravely, setting down his cup and standing. He is a tall, florid, sorrowful-looking man. "If I must, yes." He turns. "What are you writing?"

"Notes," the young reporter says.

"For what?"

"I'm not sure yet. Perhaps you might let me interview you."

"It would be good for morale," the commissar suggests. "Our men need heroes."

"Our men need boots," the division commander says. It is a constant grievance with him: the poor supply lines, the lack of reliable boots and rifles and ammunition. "Put that in your article."

The young reporter has long been drawn to men like this division commander. It is a weakness, he recognizes in himself, this fascination with power. What was it Gorky once told him? "You have a particular talent for making dangerous friends." Certainly this division commander is dangerous enough, though no friend. The young reporter has heard the rumors about him, some of them quite fantastic: that he was a priest before the revolution, a farmer of sugar beets; that he was taught to read in the crumbling trenches at Tannenberg between German artillery attacks by a Marxist who somehow saw in him the ruthless commander he would one day become; that he is the dishonored son of a general who once loyally served the now-dead tsar. The only thing known for certain is that nothing about him is truly known; home, childhood, family—all of it is kept locked away, or has been excised altogether. Instead he has rendered himself in the revolution's merciless image, and it has made him what he is: its sword. On his left hand, where the thumb and forefinger meet, is a little white scar in the shape of a bird as drawn by a child, all wings and no head. From firing a pistol, the division commander once told the young reporter.

"The man is completely without tact," the commissar later complains. They are in the kitchen with the cook's lazy-eyed helper, in a sprawling white farmhouse. It is raining outside, a sudden, gusting, summery rain. A bottle of vodka sits on the cutting block, and as the blowing rain rattles against the windows, the young reporter empties his glass and reaches for it.

"Tact or no tact, he's an excellent soldier."

"Of course." The commissar hesitates.

"But?"

"All this complaining about supplies and reinforcements. It reflects poorly on his superiors, and inevitably on the Party. A man in his position, with his potential—" The commissar lowers his voice. "He should know better. If he is to get along—politically, I mean, if he is to advance in the Party—he should know when to be quiet and simply let matters lie."

"Like you."

"No," the commissar says. "I let my opinions get away from me. You heard me back there. I'm as bad as he is. But then I don't have his authority. I'm more a standard bearer than anything." He smiles and finishes off the vodka in his glass. "Like you."

Lulled by the drumming rain, the cook's helper drowses on his feet; his boots, the young reporter notices, are falling apart. Perhaps he is dreaming of bright, well-stocked commissaries full of sturdy boots no amount of walking will ever wear out: the endless, simple harvest of riches the young reporter promised in his first article, which the cook's helper will parrot to him from time to time. It is a vision the cook's helper has succumbed to without question. In this way the young reporter envies him sometimes. He would also like to believe unquestioningly in that endless harvest.

But this cook's helper, he doubts nothing. Asked what role he intends to occupy in the new Soviet Russia, he will answer without hesitation: aviator. An absurd wish. He can barely light a stove by himself and yet he dreams of flying planes. "Tell me, what exactly does an aviator do, comrade?" some joker will invariably ask, hiding his smirk. "It is an aviator's duty to educate the peasant, to show the peasant that there are no angels or devils hiding in the clouds." This, the cook's helper insists, is essentially all aviators do, as he was himself enlightened that first bright August after the revolution by a Bolshevik pilot who flew him up over his tiny village outside Smolensk, high over the scalloped mud streets and steep-roofed huts; over the heaps of moldering trash and ugly, dark animal pens; over his barefooted neighbors out flailing wheat in the fields beside the canal where, as a boy, he watched his mother and aunts slowly, grimly hauling barges every autumn, every spring, their arms held down at their sides by great heavy straps that stretched behind them like history itself; over the only world he had ever known but had never before seen so clearly, into a sky suddenly emptied of devils and angels.

For three nights, while they await supplies in the white farmhouse, the column takes fire. It is the weakest of gestures, and as a defensive tactic, almost comical: a handful of Polish irregulars with hunting rifles shooting wildly from the woods some two hundred meters away. As soon as their fire is returned, the Poles vanish, like ghosts. On the third night, when a stray bullet strikes the wall beside the division commander's head as he stands studying his maps, the joke sours. At dawn, as the young reporter sleeps, the Cossacks ride out.

When they return hours later, they are herding half a dozen bloody, dazed-looking Poles before them through the high grass. This, the young reporter discovers, is all that remains of their attackers; the rest—some twenty men—lie scattered among the trees where they were cut down. "You should have come, scribbler," K calls happily. The gold caps on his teeth gleam fiercely, he is less circus gypsy now than grinning demon. At the edge of the field the Poles are made to strip down to their underwear—jackets, trousers, boots: the Cossacks fight each other for every scrap of clothing.

That afternoon new orders arrive: they are to keep moving, the supplies will be sent by train to R——, a week's march away. Roped together, barefooted, the Poles are told to keep up with the column or be shot.

"We are not your enemy," the commissar tells them. In his earnestness he has jumped down from the wagon to walk with the prisoners, who turn their faces from him. "This marshal of yours, this lying pig Pilsudski, he is your enemy, not Russia. It is for your good as well, our being here. We are brothers."

Brothers, the young reporter thinks. And the dead Poles sprawled in those woods back there—are they, too, his brothers? The reins dangle across his knees; the horses know enough to follow the wagon ahead of them, he thinks: let them lead us to Warsaw. Behind him, ablaze in the day's last fiery light, the cook's helper stands among his pots with the young reporter's field glasses, scanning the empty sky.

On the morning they are to advance on R—, as the division commander confers with his subordinates under the wide branches of a plum tree, planning their assault, a car drives out. From the wagon the young reporter and commissar watch the car's long tail of dust rise and spread over the dying fields.

"It seems we've been expected," the commissar murmurs.

And they have. A dignitary, an old man in a green velvet vest and coat, steps smartly from the back of the dusty sedan and presents the division commander with an official letter of surrender, signed by the town's selectmen. "Anything you require," the old man says, "anything at all. We are at your service."

"And your army?" asks the division commander.

"Fled." The old man's voice cracks. He gazes up at the plum tree, holding up a shaky hand to shade his eyes. "Yesterday. As soon as they heard you were coming. Isn't that so?" he asks his driver, turning.

"Like rabbits," the driver says.

In R— they discover a town all but untouched by the war. There are elderly couples out walking spaniels, young women carrying babies and groceries and bunches of flowers tied with twine. Children on their way home from school pause to watch the column pass, their arms laden with books. Every corner has its teahouse, its tobacconist, every shelf is crowded with cakes and pickled herring, bolts of soft linen, boots. In the bustling open-air market, in the very heart of R—, overflowing baskets of plums stand tilted toward the busy street like an invitation.

Near a park they stop. The old man bounds up the iron steps of a mansion. A maid stands at the open door, waiting. She is young, beautiful; her dark eyes gleam. She bows to them.

"Whose house is this?" the young reporter asks the old man.

"The mayor's."

"And where is he?"

"Who knows? Gone. With the rest of the trash. Anyway, he was an idiot," the old man admits sadly. Their footsteps echo, a soldier shouts joyously in the street outside, as if the war were already ended. The old man is opening one door after another, ushering the division staff from room to room; it is his way of showing them the house has no secrets. "You see?" he is saying. "Beautiful, yes?" As they linger in the parlor among the leather sofas and cut-crystal lamps, the maid appears, carrying a gleaming tray of cordials, and when they have emptied their glasses, there is brandy, there is spiced vodka, there is wine. A vision overtakes the young reporter: they are like those gaping peasants in Petrograd who wandered in stunned silence through the Winter Palace after the tsar and his doomed family fled, eager to touch everything; the mighty have fallen, the gates stand open. Anything they need, anything they have ever wanted or wished for, it is all at their fingertips. It is all theirs for the taking.

The prisoners are kept in the gated courtyard behind the new headquarters, in a garden shed. At night, while the division commander's raucous staff dines at the mayor's table, the Poles huddle among flower pots and sacks of fertilizer, quiet as stones. As they show no interest in escaping, they are allowed to move freely about the courtyard during the day and even write letters to their families, which the commissar collects regularly but does not send off. After the war, after the capital has fallen and there are no more secrets to protect, he promises the young reporter, he will give these men back their letters so they can return to their families with some record of their experience. In this way their wives and children will one day learn of the kindness with which they were treated by their captors, and the revolution will flourish.

"You're joking," says the young reporter.

One day the cook's helper asks the young reporter, "When are we going to see something new from you?" They are handing the prisoners their evening ration: a slice of coarse black bread, a slice of onion.

"Soon," the young reporter tells him.

All week now he has watched these Poles accept their meager portion of black bread and onion without complaint, and all week, every day, he has at odd moments found himself remembering his dream of Petrograd: the unseen circling airplane, the falling pamphlets, the parade of banners along the black, ice-locked Neva. With his notebook and pencil, he spends his afternoons exploring R—, scratching notes that have become, without his realizing it, a kind of journal. He is saving all of it: the vibrant, noisy market, the teahouses with their bright awnings, the well-stocked shops. Is this the heaven of simple riches he was imagining when he wrote that article for *Red Cavalrymen*? Is this their reward?

One night, drunk on the mayor's dry champagne, he stumbles out to the garden shed. Behind him the mansion blazes with lamps, with music—another party is in full swing. One of the panes of glass set in the shed door is partially broken out, and as he leans heavily against the locked door, trying to peer inside, the mayor's mansion trembles in the crescent of glass like a palace of light in a fairy tale.

"Brothers," he calls softly. "I've not forgotten you. See?" He pushes the piece of glass out and slips the half-empty champagne bottle through the hole, as a gift, an offering. "For you," he says. The little garden shed breathes its sharp black odor of turned earth and fertilizer into his face, his hand hangs in darkness. A grave, he suddenly thinks. I am reaching into a grave.

Later, after the party has broken up, he finds the cook's helper passed out in a crowded hallway upstairs and shakes him awake. "What is it?" the cook's helper mumbles thickly; his lazy left eye, unmoored, drifts past the young reporter's face.

"Why is it so important that you become an aviator?" asks the young reporter. "Aren't you happy? Isn't being a cook's helper enough?"

"No."

"Listen to me," the young reporter says. "You think I know anything? What if you never get to fly airplanes? What if I was wrong? What if I was lying? About everything."

"You're weren't lying."

"How can you be so sure?"

The cook's helper blinks. "I trust you," he says, and rolls over.

They are ordered west again, back into the war. "You look disappointed," the commissar tells the young reporter. They are the last to leave the mayor's mansion, which after two weeks has begun to resemble nothing so much as a badly managed hotel: the furniture is in shambles, the crystal lamps shattered. The dark-eyed maid, whom the young reporter has several times caught sneaking drinks for herself, whom he has watched slip away with K one night and another soldier the next, bows as they pass her in the hallway by the front door, but there is something slightly corrupt in the gesture now.

"Do I?" asks the young reporter.

Four days west of R—, as the young reporter sits drowsing on the wagon bench, the Poles finally attack. Terrified, the cook's helper whips the horses mercilessly, shouting, trying to turn them around even as K and the other Cossacks fly past with their drawn swords flashing, straight at the Polish machine guns. The bleached sky rattles and snaps like sheet metal in a storm, the fields leap up in black fountains around them.

"They've dug in," the division commander announces that night, drawing his hand across the map. "What a fucking nightmare. Two weeks ago we could have rolled over them in a matter of hours."

"And now?" asks the young reporter.

"Now—" The division commander does not look up. The white, bird-shaped scar on his outspread hand is luminous; the young reporter's gaze follows it across the map. "We begin paying for ground."

Late the next morning, with his notebook and pencil, the young reporter creeps through the woods with the cook's helper. They are going to the front. The cook's helper carries half a dozen canteens slung round his shoulders; all morning he has been tirelessly bringing the soldiers their water this way. As he and the young reporter are crossing a small clearing, a shell bursts high in the treetops to their left, showering the grass with shrapnel, knocking them both flat. It all happens so fast that the young reporter is on his feet again and running before he even realizes it. He discovers he is alone. Retracing his steps, he finds the cook's helper slumped against the trunk of a pine tree beside the clearing, in a pool of flickering sunlight. "I tripped," the cook's helper slurs. The back of his head is wet; the shoulders of his coarse tunic, into which the leather straps of the heavy canteens bite, is soaked through, sodden with blood. Groaning, the young reporter hauls him to his feet and starts back toward camp.

"You forgot me."

The cook's helper is smiling sleepily, as if at some secret joke.

"Just at first," the young reporter says.

In no time at all they are lost. The young reporter is gasping, he has forgotten the way back. In the distance, as they stand resting by a rotting log they have passed twice already, they hear a whistle sounding the assault. "We have to leave the canteens," he tells the cook's helper. "I can barely carry you as it is. I'll come back for them later. I promise."

"You won't forget?"

"No," says the young reporter, "I won't forget."

Headquarters is a country unto itself. Twice already they have had to abandon the rotting farmhouse they now occupy in order to avoid being overrun by the Poles, who themselves were forced to flee the farmhouse only yesterday. There are papers scattered in every room: requisition receipts, postcards, unfinished letters in Polish, in Russian. *You and our daughters are in my prayers and in my dreams. I embrace you.* At night the walls leak wind, the sagging roof gapes, the young reporter can see the stars winking through as he lies sleepless in his little corner, among soldiers. In the other room the division commander paces before his maps, dictating orders in a low growl no one else dares talk above, so that when his staff speaks they speak in whispers. All their easy hopes for a quick return home have evaporated. There are rumors of impending counterattack, talk of stalemate. All across Europe, everywhere they turn, walls are going up. England, it is reported, is sending guns and advisors by the trainload into White-occupied Russia. Kerensky plots an invasion from his exile in Paris, while their leaders in Moscow bicker and conspire among themselves for power.

In Berlin, Rosa Luxemburg weeps as she is dragged from the opulent lobby of the Hotel Eden to a waiting car, only to be later dredged from Landwehr Canal like some moldering relic from a scuttled ship. History has abandoned them.

"No devils," the cook's helper tells the young reporter. They are in the barn behind the rotting farmhouse, among the wounded, the dying. After days of drifting in and out of consciousness, the cook's helper has begun to hallucinate. Smolensk, the wheat falling before the whistling flail, the groaning barge straps tight around his mother. "I looked," he murmurs, and for a moment his wandering weak eye ceases its roaming, for a moment it finds the young reporter's face. "You were wrong. There's nothing up there." The smell of smoke carries across the farmyard. The dreaming horses stir uneasily in their stalls. A barn swallow darts among the darkening rafters overhead as night comes on, building its nest.

A week later they are sent back to R—: the young reporter, the commissar, K. They have outrun their communication lines, and are under orders to requisition more telegraph wire. The Polish front has collapsed, the victorious column continues its march west, gathering prisoners as it goes. Repeatedly the commissar must pull the wagon off the road in order to allow by reinforcements from Kiev: Cossacks, black-booted commissars, machine gunners sprawled atop tachankas in the merciless sun. "Good luck, children!" K calls from the back of the wagon, waving a bottle. He has been drunk for days, ever since his beautiful horse was shot out from under him. Without his horse he is useless. In the distance a loose funnel of crows rises and swirls over the desolate plain like burning paper.

A young officer approaches and demands their papers.

"Who're you?" asks K.

The young officer's hand rests on his pistol. "Cheka."

He has the face of an angel. They wait as their orders are checked, their names recorded. The blazing sun beats down. The crows circle. Waiting, the young reporter finds himself remembering his dream of Petrograd. He stands at the window, watching the leaflets flutter down. *Everything we ever cherished, we have given. But rejoice!* Soon, he thinks, the hidden plane will reveal itself, the door will shudder on its hinges. He will hear his name shouted, he will hear them calling for him. *Babel!*

"Keep moving," the young officer says, handing back their orders.

It is dark when they finally reach R—. A young girl in white stockings skips past, counting the steps between the gas lamps under her breath. The bright shops beckon, the packed teahouses have opened their tall windows to the mild evening air. Joyous laughter rings over the market, where the baskets will always be full. They are on a wide, level street lined, it seems, with nothing but churches. More than anything, the young reporter would like to stop and rest, if only for a moment, if only long enough to forget the war for a little while. But already the wagon is lurching forward.

"Wake up, child," K whispers in his ear, shaking him. "We've arrived."

ALEX KUO

Free Kick

A girth for pack or saddle; a tight grip;
a thing done with ease; a certainty to happen.
—Webster's for *cinch*

Two years had slipped by since Cinch moved into the interior to be closer to the projects where he did most of his work, but mostly Cinch was here because this was where he wanted to be. While cracking two eggs into the pan over a low propane flame, he counted the number of deliveries he was scheduled to make this morning, five or six. Would there be enough amoxicillin much needed by the children this time of year, with or without bubblegum flavoring? He scrunched his eyes, and wondered if such foreign invasion of their immune system was fair trade for the destruction of their traditional diet. Would he be back in time for the meeting with the Minister of Natural Resources and Environment?

It had taken him five months of continuous effort to set her up for this meeting. He never had any doubt about it, though in a challenging moment last month he thought about acquiring a religion for once, just to help it along. But he didn't, and chose instead to focus his energies on getting something done rather than debating over things he could not prove.

He spooned the scrambled eggs onto a porcelain plate and ate standing up. What he could prove was that it could be done. After all, he was used to seeing the seemingly impossible reverse itself in his own country, a country of flimflams and cons in which people willingly believed that dropping a uranium-235 bomb and a plutonium-239 bomb on civilians that indiscriminately killed two hundred and eighty thousand people instantly half a century ago actually saved lives. For emphasis, he scraped a thumbnail across the copper rivets of his porcelain plate. So, in a series of increasingly detailed and provocative letters and e-mails to the Natural Resources and Environment Minister, he added to his daily diet of four hundred lies, on the average. And why not?

Cinch's first letter politely requested a meeting at the Minister's convenience, suggesting that since the two of them had a mutual interest in the continued welfare of the some three hundred square miles of natural preserve owned by the government—two hundred thousand acres or roughly half the size of the county in Oregon that Cinch grew up in—they meet to discuss developing some plans for maintaining its ecological integrity. Each subsequent letter and e-mail prompted more discussion items: reforestation and erosion control; protection for the flora and fauna, and, of course, including the frogs and cicadas; water conservation and safeguards for water quality; the e-mails in the last month attaching as documents a copy of his graduate degree in forestry, and experience testimonials for fire management and recreation work with the U.S. Forest Service; and the final letter exploring a mutually beneficial program proffering the eleven small villages that ring the lower elevations of this park as a buffer zone against commercial development. Whew! Take that, kiddo. All but where to put the crapper. How could she refuse?

Quatar knocked and came into the kitchen, pouring himself a cup of cold coffee before asking, "Hey, ready?"

Dark-skinned with deep, dark brown eyes suggesting impatience, it was Quatar's final touch in getting a sympathetic friend at the embassy to invite the Minister to a cultural exchange reception two weeks ago where they met at last face-to-face and agreed to this afternoon's meeting. He had also helped Cinch with many of the items on the shopping list sent to M.N.R.E. After all, he had grown up in one of these eleven villages before he went to the city for an education hundreds of miles away on the coast. Now he was back years later, for just about the same reasons that Cinch was here from thousands of miles away.

"Hey, yeah. How many—" Cinch started to ask.

Quatar held up the extended fingers of his right hand, a throwback to their early days of working together for a relief organization and fumbling with the language. Cinch knew that Quatar's eyes saw and remembered everything, everything, and suspected that if his friend would one day turn to writing, he would be merciless. "The sixth clinic is closed today. They took someone to the city's hospital last night—not bad, a field cut. The barefoot nurse did her job. We have enough amoxi for this morning."

* * *

The meeting took place at a former sweatshop the local municipal government in partnership with a civilian action team and the foreign assistance program that Cinch and Quatar worked for took over a couple of years ago. This building had been abandoned two years ago by the garment-manufacturing owners when its workers, women all, unionized and submitted a list of demands to the management. Now, in stepped the Minister of Natural Resources and Environment. Cinch saw her as a quick blonde with double-lined lips, someone misplaced in time and location, or worse. Followed by several aides, she sat uncomfortably on a bench in the former factory that now served as a training center for the villages' barefoot nurses who sometimes also took charge of their domestic violence and children's health care programs.

"You like my rings, no," the Minister asked when she saw Cinch staring at her hands with a ring on every finger, including the thumbs. "Each one is a stone from a different province of the country," she explained.

It dawned on Cinch that while he had some answers, the Minister did not know what the questions were. He looked over at Quatar, who seemed to be fighting sleep or shutting his eyes in impatience. Shrugging his shoulders, he was no help.

"Thank you for coming here," Cinch started saying, first making sure that everyone had a seat and a cold soft drink in front of them. Having heard about the government's emphasis on its need for transparency, he said, "To be quick, I'm proposing that you transfer the maintenance of this natural preserve to our organization."

Silence, followed by more silence. The Minister was not looking at him.

She sipped on her straw, then said, "You do not have the resources to do it," looking directly at Cinch, emphasizing every word.

"Nor do you," Cinch looked right back at her.

"I have a proposition," he added. "We'll turn this nature preserve into a park with interpretative center, cabins, restaurant, and trails. We'll take care of it."

"Wait, wait, wait," interrupted a woman with a baby in the back of the hall. She had stood up and was gesturing with her free hand. "What are we supposed to say to these tourists as we walk them along the trail? Ask them 'Are you enjoying our country today?' We have a shortage of everything. When will we have time to entertain the tourists?" She then asked if anyone wondered who would clean their toilets and trim their hedges.

Another woman stood up, too, and said, "We don't have a shortage of nothing."

Several people laughed, including Quatar, who was avoiding Cinch's searching look on what to say next.

Cinch was facing a dilemma here. Since Shrub had been residing at 1600 Pennsylvania Avenue, his country's compliant news media had served as the middle-class's firewall against radical doubt. And why not? The children of the Baby Boomer generation had swarmed to the schools' communications programs, and now as journalists, reporters, columnists, anchors, even boom operators, they were on the job. Their visuals compressed time and space, past and present, and with changing images every two seconds and close-ups eliminating cause-and-effect, the viewer walked away with a dizzying montage of impressions signifying nothing in particular. Yes, yes, change the image, make it up, add more pixels, a lot easier than changing the real thing. Cinch sensed this was the turning moment at the meeting, but he was not exactly prepared for it happening so fast.

"Yes, that's all very true," he said, looking at the two women in the back of the room. Then he looked straight at Quatar. While he still had doubts if three hundred square miles were sufficient to sustain its biological integrity against encroaching airborne and underground seepage of toxic industrial waste, it was a bit late to back out now. But there was a chance, as there was a mountain range running through the middle of the preserve. "I propose that we play a ninety-minute soccer game," he said. "Between your Ministry and these villages. The winner will take control of the park."

The Minister looked up, and her assistant leaned over and whispered something to her.

"That's impossible. You can't be serious."

"Yes, I am."

Cinch stood up and added, "Your Ministry doesn't have any

funds to do it, the World Bank and I.M.F. want you to privatize it, and in the meantime nothing's being done."

He believed in his convictions, and damn it, he wasn't going to let the strengths of the Peace Corps, World Vision, Mercy Corps, Oxfam, Doctors Without Borders, or even Opus Dei stop him from doing what needed to be done in wrangling control of this piece of land from the benign government. The villagers would relearn how to care for it as they'd done for centuries, with adjustments for compass and tack, and in return be nourished by it before the Americans seized it and developed it into a destination resort in its harvest of empire.

"This is highly unusual," the Minister said, looking at her assistant. "There is no protocol for this."

Quatar raised a hand and held up five fingers. "A trial period. Let's agree that if we win, we'll have it for a five-year trial period."

The Minister and her assistant looked at the half dozen villagers gathered at the edge of the hall, looking at their shoes, sizing up their chances.

"And what if you lose?" she asked, smiling for the only time that afternoon.

Before Cinch or Quatar could say anything, the smarty-pants woman in the back yelled out, "We've already lost everything."

But they all knew that they didn't want to lose the same thing twice.

*   *   *

So this was it, this empty schoolyard on Sunday, except for a few neighborhood kids curious about the gathering of fancy vans, pickups, and sedans from the city. The Ministry's team of some twenty players had on new Adidas white and blue uniforms and matching shoes, accompanied by their own referee with whistle and two linesmen. Cinch knew they were not really enemy, but they sure looked like it with their intimidating warm-up drills. This was only a game, though the stakes were high, at least for us, Cinch thought. On his annual visits with his family in Oregon, Cinch had felt more space slipping in between him and that community in which he had spent the first eighteen years of his life, its excesses and self-indulgence displayed for all to see on Friday nights finding its way here on this Sunday.

The Minister walked over to where Cinch was stretching, her

hands on her waist, acting astonished, that outraged school-teacher pose.

"You can't play, you're not eligible, you're not a villager," she challenged.

"Why not?" Cinch looked over to the two Peace Corps volunteers dressed in white and blue. "What about them?" In fact he had met one of them before, a gal from Muncie, Indiana, who was a striker on the championship Northwestern team last year. "If they are eligible, so am I." Cinch had always been curious about these Peace Corps volunteers. Here they were, seventy percent of them liberal arts majors. They came loaded with morality but no life skills except for doing e-mails, jogging, and soccer. "And besides, we're one player short."

"Okay, okay." The Minister flashed her eyes. "Since this is a friendly game, you can borrow one of ours. We have enough."

Cinch looked over at Quatar, who agreed with him. No way, no defector, turncoat, expat, DP, or, worse, a mole, especially on loan. What would be the interest? Who could trust his motive in error or valor?

*　*　*

It was a slow endurance game. Except for the two Peace Corps volunteers, the first half exhausted every player, including the two goalies. The score was tied 0–0 after a penalty-free forty-five minutes, as no side could put together a coordinated offense of more than twenty yards or two consecutive passes, whichever was less. Both teams were stretched out on the sidelines drinking water. Cinch and Quatar looked around at their teammates. They wanted to say something encouraging, wave a flag or cheer or something, but they both knew that nothing more was needed to motivate them.

So the second half continued like the first, and several times both goalies left their penalty area to join the offense. Not many players were running anymore. Even when someone had the ball or was marking the person with the ball, it was all in slow motion. Most were visibly panting, hands on waists, and, whenever possible, bent over and sucking air.

Well close to the very last seconds of the game, a short villager with peddling cucumber legs managed to dribble the ball all by himself past the last white and blue defender, including the out-of-position goalie, who had huffed his way up to midfield in an all-out last-minute suicide squeeze. The villager had the ball all to himself and was headed straight for the goal, until the only person still able to catch up with him, that Peace Corps gal from Muncie, Indiana, made an illegal sliding tackle from the rear in the penalty zone, sending both the ball and player to the side of the goal. Instantly the shrill whistle went up, a penalty-kick call with about five seconds left in the game.

The Minister screamed and protested the call, but there was no doubt it was to be a penalty kick.

Who would take it? Who had a strong and straight kick?

"I'll take it." It was Quatar, and it was the moment he had been waiting for. "Twelve steps out, right? I'll take it."

So it had come down to this. Eighty-nine minutes in which nothing much of anything happened, and now, the whistle, the red card, and a free kick that would almost always score, in this case, winning the game. Except for Quatar and the goalie, both sides had lined up behind the ball, witnesses to the one-on-one. He moved quickly toward the ball from the right, faked a hard kick that was followed by the diving goalie, and with his left heel behind him, Quatar tapped the ball into the net, a trick shot he had learned in grade school decades ago. That was it. End of game. Wild screaming and cheering. "We got it back" was repeated again and again, at least for the next five years.

The Princess of Nebraska

Sasha wished that she would never have to see Boshen again after this trip. She ran to the bathroom the moment they entered the McDonald's, leaving him to order for them both. He had suggested a good meal in Chinatown, and she had refused. She wanted to see downtown Chicago before going to the clinic at Planned Parenthood the next morning. It was the only reason for her to ride the Greyhound bus all day from Nebraska. Kansas City would have been a wiser choice, closer, cheaper, but there was nothing to see there—the trip was not meant for sightseeing, but Sasha hoped to get at least something out of it. She did not want to spend all her money only to remember a drugged sleep in a dreary motel in the middle of nowhere. Sasha had grown up in a small town in Inner Mongolia; vast and empty landscapes depressed her.

"You must be tired," Boshen said as he pushed the tray of food to Sasha, who had taken a table by the window. She looked tiny in the oversized sweatshirt. Her face was slightly swollen, and the way she checked out the customers in the store, her eyes staying on each face a moment too long, moved him. She was twenty-one, a child still.

"I got a fish sandwich for you," Boshen said when Sasha did not answer him.

"I haven't seen one happy face since arriving," Sasha said. "What's the other one?"

"Chicken."

Sasha threw the fish sandwich across the table and grabbed the chicken sandwich from Boshen's tray. "I hate fish," she said.

"It's good for you now," Boshen said.

"Now will be over soon," Sasha said. She looked forward to the moment when she would be ready to move on. Moving on was a phrase she had just learned, an American concept that suited her well. It was such a wonderful phrase that Sasha could almost see herself stapling her Chinese life, one staple after another, around the pages until they became one solid block that nobody would be able to open and read. She would have a fresh page then, for her American life. She was four months late already.

Boshen said nothing and unwrapped the fish sandwich. It was a change—sitting at a table and having an ordered meal—after months of eating in the kitchen of the Chinese restaurant where he worked as a helper to the Sichuan chef. Boshen had come to America via a false marriage to a friend five months earlier, when he had been put under house arrest for his correspondence with a western reporter regarding a potential AIDS epidemic in a central province. He had had to publish a written confession of his wrong-doing to earn his freedom. A lesbian friend, a newly naturalized American citizen herself, had offered to marry him out of China for his safety. Before that, he had lived an openly gay life in Beijing, madly in love with Yang, an eighteen-year-old boy. Boshen had tried different ways to contact Yang since he had arrived in America, but the boy never responded. The checks Boshen sent him were not cashed, either.

They ate without speaking. Sasha swallowed her food fast and waited for Boshen to finish his. Outside the window, more and more people appeared, all moving towards the downtown, red reindeer's antlers on the heads of children who sat astride on their fathers' shoulders. Boshen saw the question in Sasha's eyes, and told her that there was a parade that evening, and all the trees on Michigan Avenue would light up for the coming Thanksgiving and Christmas holidays. "Do you want to stay for it?" he asked halfheartedly, hoping that she would choose instead to rest after the long bus ride.

"Why not?" Sasha said, and put on her coat.

Boshen folded the sandwich wrapper like a freshly ironed napkin. "I wonder if we could talk for a few minutes here," he said.

Sasha sighed. She had never liked Boshen, whom she had met only once. He had struck her as the type of man who was as fussy as an old hen. She had not hesitated, however, to call him and ask for help when she had found out his number through an acquaintance. She had spoken in a dry, matter-of-fact way about her pregnancy that had gone too long for an abortion in the state of Nebraska. Yang had fathered the baby, she had told Boshen during their first phone call. She had had no intention of sparing

Boshen the truth; in a way, she felt Boshen was responsible for her misfortune, too.

"Have you, uh, made up your mind about the operation?" Boshen asked.

"What do you think I'm here for?" Sasha said. Over the past week Boshen had called her twice, bringing up the possibility of keeping the baby. Both times she had hung up right away. Whatever interest he had in the baby was stupid and selfish, Sasha had decided.

The easiest solution may not be the best one in life, Boshen thought of telling Sasha, but then, what right did he have to talk about options, when the decisions he had made for his life were all compromises? At thirty-eight, Boshen felt he had achieved less than he had failed. He had been a mediocre doctor before he was asked politely to leave the hospital for establishing the first counseling hotline for homosexuals in the small Chinese city where he lived. He moved to Beijing and took on a part-time job at a private clinic while working as an activist for gay rights. After a few visits from the secret police, however, he realized that, in the post-Tiananmen era, talk of any kind of human rights was dangerous. He decided to go into a less extreme and more practical area, advocating for AIDS awareness, but even that he had to give up after pressure from the secret police and his family. He was in love with a boy twenty years younger, and he thought he could make a difference to the boy's life. In the end, he was the one to marry a woman and leave. Boshen had thought of adopting the baby—half of her blood came from Yang, after all—but Sasha's eyes, sharp and unrelenting, chilled him. He smiled weakly and said, "I just wanted to make sure."

Sasha wrapped her head in a shawl and stood up. Boshen did not move, and when she asked him if he was leaving, he said, "I've heard from my friends that Yang is prostituting again."

Not a surprise, Sasha thought, but the man at the table, too old for a role as a heartbroken lover and too serious for it, was pitiful. In a kinder voice she said, "Then we'll have to live with that, no?"

Boshen was not the first man to have fallen in love with Yang, but he believed, for a long time, that he was the only one to have seen and touched the boy's soul. Since the age of seven, Yang had been trained as a *Nan Dan*—a male actor who plays female roles on stage in the Peking Opera—and had lived his life in the Opera school. At seventeen, when he was discovered going out with a male lover, he was expelled. Boshen had written several articles about the incident, but he had not met Yang until he had become a money boy. Yang could've easily enticed a willing man to keep him for a good price, but rumors were that the boy was only interested in selling after his first lover had abandoned him.

The day Boshen heard about Yang's falling into prostitution, he went to the park where men paid for such services. It was near dusk when he arrived, and men of all ages slipped into the park like silent fishes. Soon night fell; beneath the lampposts, transactions started in whispers, familiar scenarios for Boshen, but standing in the shade of a tree—a customer instead of researcher—made him tremble. It was not difficult to recognize Yang in the moon-white colored silk shirt and pants he was reputed to wear every day to the park. Boshen watched the boy, too beautiful for the grimy underground, a white lotus blossom untouched by the surrounding mud.

After watching the boy for several days, Boshen finally offered to pay Yang's asking price. The night Yang came home with him, Boshen became drunk on his own words. For a long time he talked about his work, his dream of bringing an end to injustice and building a more tolerant world; Yang huddled on the couch and listened. Boshen thought of shutting up, but the more he talked, the more he despaired at the beautiful and impassive face of Yang—in the boy's eyes he must have been the same as all the other men, so full of themselves. Finally, Boshen said, "Someday I'll make you go back to the stage."

"*An empty promise of a man keeps a woman's heart full,*" Yang recited in a low voice.

"But this," Boshen said, pointing to the pile of paperwork on his desk. "This is the work that will make it illegal for them to take you away from the stage because of who you are."

Yang's face softened. Boshen watched the unmistakable hope in the boy's eyes. Yang was too young to hide his pain, despite years of wearing female masks and portraying other women's pains onstage, and Boshen wanted to save him from his suffering. After a few weeks of pursuing, Boshen convinced Yang to try a new life.

Boshen redecorated the apartment with expensive, hand-painted curtains that featured the costumes of the Peking Opera and huge paper lanterns bearing the Peking Opera masks. He sold a few pieces of furniture to make space and borrowed a rug from a friend for Yang to practice on. Yang fit into the quiet life like the most virtuous woman he had played onstage. He got up early every morning, stretching his body into unbelievable positions and dancing the most intricate choreography. He trained his voice, too, in the shower so that the neighbors would not hear him. Always Boshen stood outside and listened, Yang's voice splitting the waterfall, the bath curtain, the door, and the rest of the dull world like a silver knife. At those moments, Boshen was overwhelmed by gratitude—he was not the only one to have been touched by the boy's beauty, but he was the one to guard and nurture it. That alone lifted him above his mundane, disappointing life.

When Boshen was at work, Yang practiced painting and calligraphy—they had been taught to him in the Opera School. Sometimes they went out to parties, but most evenings they stayed home, quiet and uneventful. Yang never performed for Boshen, and he dared not ask him to. Yang was an angel falling out of the heaven, and every day Boshen dreaded that he would not be able to return the boy to where he belonged.

Such a fear, as it turned out, was not unreasonable. Two months into the relationship, Yang started to show signs of restlessness. During the day he went out more than before, and he totally abandoned painting and calligraphy. Boshen wondered if the boy was suffocated by the stillness of their life.

One day shortly before Boshen was expelled from Beijing and put under house arrest in his hometown, Yang asked him casually how his work was going. Fine, Boshen said, feeling uneasy. Yang had never asked him anything about his work; it was part of the ugly world that Boshen had wanted to shelter Yang from.

"What are you working on?" Yang asked.

"Why, the usual stuff," Boshen said.

"I heard you were working on AIDS," Yang said. "What has that to do with you?"

Stunned, Boshen tried to find an explanation. Finally, he said, "You don't understand, Yang."

"I'm not a child," Yang said. "Why are you concerned with that dirty disease? The more you work on it, the more people will connect it with gay people. What good does it do for us?"

"I'm trying to help more people than the two of us," Boshen said.

"But you've promised to help me get back to the stage," Yang said. "If you insist on working on something irrelevant, you'll never fulfill your promise."

Boshen could not answer Yang. Afterwards, Yang started to go out more often, and a few days later, he did not come home for the first time in their relationship. Boshen thought of all the predators waiting to pounce on Yang, and he did not sleep for the night.

"There's nothing for you to worry about," Yang said with a strange smile when Boshen confronted him. "I'm not as endangered as you imagine."

"At least you should've let me know where you were," Boshen said.

"I was with a girl," Yang said, and mentioned a name, Sasha, that sounded slightly familiar to Boshen. They had met her at a party, Yang reminded Boshen, but he did not remember who she was; he did not understand why Yang was going out with her.

"Why? What a silly question," Yang said. "You do things when you feel like it, no?"

The first time Sasha met Yang at a party, she felt that she was looking into a mirror that reflected not her own face, but that of someone she could never become. She watched the ballet of his long fingers across the table while he listened absentmindedly to the conversation of others around the table. She looked at the innocent half moons on his fingernails; her own fingers were plump and blunt. His cream-colored face, his delicate nose and mouth reminded her of an exquisite china doll. Later, when they sat closer, she saw the melancholy in his eyes, and decided that he was more like a statue of *Kuanyin*, the male Buddha in a female body, the goddess who listened and responded to the prayers of suffering women and children. In front of him, Sasha felt like a mass-produced rubber doll.

The uneasy feeling lasted only for a moment. Sasha had heard stories about him, and was glad to see him finally in person. She leaned toward him and asked, as if picking up from a conversation they had dropped somewhere, "What do you think of girls, then?"

He looked up at her, and she saw a strange light in his eyes. They reminded her of a wounded sparrow she had once kept during a cold Mongolian winter. Sparrows were an obstinate species that would never eat or drink once they were caged, her mother told her. Sasha did not believe it. She locked the bird for days, and it kept bumping into the cage until its head started to go bald. Still she refused to release it, mesmerized by its eyes, wild but helplessly tender, too. She nudged the little bowl of soaked millet closer to the sparrow, but the bird was blind to her hospitality. Cheap birds, a neighbor told her; only cheap birds would be so stubborn. Have a canary, the neighbor said, and she would be singing for you every morning by now.

The boy lowered his eyes at Sasha's scrutiny, and she felt the urge to chase the beautiful eyes, a huntress of that strange light. "You must have known some girls, no?" she said. "When you went to the Opera School, were there girls in the school?"

"Yes," the boy said, his voice reminding her of a satin dress.

"So?"

"We didn't talk. They played handmaids and nannies, background roles."

"So you were the princess, huh?" Sasha laughed, and saw the boy blush, with anger perhaps, but it made her more curious and insistent in cornering him. "What's your name?" she said.

"Which name?"

"How many names do you have?"

"Two. One given by my parents. One given by the Opera School."

"What are they?"

He dipped one finger into a glass of orange juice and wrote on the dark marble tabletop. She followed the wet trace of his finger. It was Yang, a common boy's name with the character for the sun, the masculine principle of nature, the opposite of Yin.

"A so-so name. What's your Opera name?"

"Sumeng," he said. A serene and pure dreamer, it meant.

"Worse. Sounds like a weepy name from a romance novel," Sasha said. "You need a better name. I'll have to think of one for you."

In the end, she did not use either name, and did not find a better one for him. She called him my little *Nan Dan,* and that was what he was to her, a boy destined to play a woman's part. She paged him often, and invited him to movies and walks in the park. She made decisions for them both, and he let her. She tried to pry him open with questions—she was so curious about him—and slowly he started to talk, about the man he had loved and men who loved him. He never said anything about the Opera School or his stage life, and she learned not to push him. He was so vain, Sasha thought, when he spent a long time fixing his hair or when he put on an expression of aloofness at the slightest attention of a stranger; she teased him, and then felt tender and guilty when he did not defend himself. She made fun of the other people in Yang's life, too, his lover, Boshen, whom she believed to be a useless dreamer, and the men who boldly asked him for his number. She believed she was the first person in his life who did not worship him in any way, and he must have followed her around because of that. It pleased her.

Was she dating the boy? Sasha's classmates asked when they saw her with Yang more than once. Of course not, she said. In a month, Sasha was to go to America for graduate school, and it was pointless to start a relationship now. Besides, how smart was it to date a boy who loved no one but himself?

Even the wind could not cut through the warm bodies lined up on both sides of Michigan Avenue. Sasha pushed through the crowd. They looked so young and carefree, these Americans, happy as a group of pupils on a field trip. She envied these people who would stand in a long line in front of a popcorn shop waiting for a bag of fresh popcorn, lovers leaning into each other, children hanging on to their parents. They were born to be themselves, naïve and contented with their naïvety.

"I would trade my place with any one of them," Sasha said to Boshen, but when he raised his voice and asked her to repeat her words, she shook her head. If only there were a law in America binding her to where her baby belonged, so that the baby would have a reason to live!

Sasha herself had once been used by the law to trap her mother in the grassland. One of the thousands of high school students sent down from Beijing to Inner Mongolia for labor reeducation, her mother, in order to join the Party, married a Mongolian herdsman, one of the model interracial marriages that were broadcast across the grassland. Five years later, at the end of the Cultural Revolution, all of the students were allowed to return to Beijing. Sasha's mother, however, was forced to stay, even after she divorced her Mongolian husband. Their two daughters, born in the grassland, did not have legal residency in Beijing, and the mother had to stay where the children belonged.

Sasha pushed forward, looking at every store window. Silky scarves curved around the mannequins' necks with soft obedience. Diamonds glistened on dark velvet. At a street corner, children gathered and watched the animated story displayed in the windows of Marshall Field's. If only her baby were a visa that would admit her into this prosperity, Sasha thought, saddened by the memories of Nebraska and Inner Mongolia, the night skies for both places black with lonely, lifeless stars.

"There's an open spot there," Boshen said. "Do you want to stand there?"

Sasha nodded, and Boshen followed her. Apart from the brief encounter at the party in Beijing and a few phone calls, he did not know her. He had thought about her often after she had called him about the pregnancy. What kind of girl, he had wondered, would've made Yang a father? He had imagined a mature and understanding girl. Beautiful, too. He had made up a perfect woman for Yang and for his own peace of mind, but Sasha had disappointed him. When they settled along the curb, he said, "So, what's your plan after the operation?"

Sasha stood on tiptoes like a child and looked in the direction where the parade would start. Boshen regretted right away speaking with such animosity. Seeing nothing, she turned to him and said, "What's *your* plan in America? Where's your new wife, anyway?"

Boshen frowned. He had told Yang that the marriage would be used as a cover, and his departure was only meant to be a temporary one. He had promised Yang other things, too, money he would send, help he would seek in the overseas Chinese community for Yang's return to the stage. Not a day since he had arrived did he forget his promises, but Sasha's words stung him. His marriage must have been an unforgivable betrayal, in Sasha's and Yang's eyes alike. "I can't defend myself," Boshen said finally.

"Of course not. You were the one sending him back to the street," Sasha said.

"It's been a troubled time," Boshen said, struggling over the words. "It's been difficult for all of us. But we certainly should try to help him out."

Sasha turned to look at Boshen with an amused smile. "You speak like the worst kind of politician," she said. "Show me the solution."

"I am thinking," Boshen said, then paused. "I've been thinking—if we can tell him that he'll be able to perform in America, maybe he would want to leave Beijing?"

"And then?"

"We will try here. There's a *Nan Dan* master in New York. Maybe we can contact him and ask for his help. But the first thing we do is to get Yang out of the country."

"Does that we include me?"

"If you could marry Yang, he would be here in no time. I know him. If there's one percent chance to go back to stage, he'll try."

"A very nice plan, Boshen," Sasha said. "But why should I agree to the proposal? What's in it for me?"

Boshen looked away from Sasha and watched a couple kiss at the other side of the street. After a long moment, he turned to Sasha and tried to look into her eyes. "You must have loved him at least once, Sasha," he said, his voice trembling.

Sasha had not planned for love, or even an affair. The friendship was out of whimsy, a convenience for the empty days immediately before graduating from college. The movie they watched one night in July was not planned, either. It was ten o'clock when Sasha purchased the tickets, at the last minute. Yang looked at the clock in the ticket booth and wondered aloud if it was too late, and Sasha laughed, asking him if he was a child, and if his lover had a curfew for him.

The movie was *Pretty Woman*, with almost unreadable Chinese subtitles. When they came out to the midnight street, Sasha said, "Don't you love Julie Roberts?"

"What's to love about her?" Yang said.

Sasha glanced at Yang. He had been quiet throughout the movie—he did not understand English, but Sasha thought at least he could've enjoyed the beautiful actress. "She's pretty, and funny, and so—American," Sasha said. "America is a good place. Everything could happen there. A prostitute becomes a princess; a crow turns into a swan overnight."

"A prostitute never becomes a princess," Yang said.

"How do you know?" Sasha said. "If only you could come with me to America and take a look at it yourself."

After a long moment, Yang said, "Every place is a good place. Only time goes wrong."

Sasha said nothing. She did not want to spend the night philosophizing. When they walked past a small hotel, she asked Yang if he wanted to come in with her. Just for the fun of staying out for a night, she said; he needn't have to report to his lover, anyway, she added. Yang hesitated, and she grabbed his hand and pulled him into the foyer with her. A middle-aged woman at the reception opened the window and said, "What do you want?"

"Comrade, do you have a single room for two persons?" Sasha said.

The woman threw out a pad for registration and shut the window. Sasha filled in the form. The woman scanned the pad. "Your ID?" she asked.

Sasha handed her ID to the woman. The woman looked at it for a long time, and pointed to Yang with her chin. "His ID?"

"He's my cousin from Inner Mongolia," Sasha said in a cheerful voice. "He forgot to bring his ID with him."

"Then there's no room tonight." The woman threw out Sasha's ID and closed the window.

"Comrade." Sasha tapped on the glass.

The woman opened the window and said, "Go away. Your cousin? Let me tell you—either you have a marriage license and I will give you a room, or you go out, do that shameless thing in the street, and let the cops arrest you. Don't you think I don't know girls like you."

Sasha dragged Yang out of the door, his lips quavering. "I don't believe I can't find a room for us," Sasha said finally.

Yang looked at Sasha, baffled. "Why do we have to do this?" he said.

"Ha, you're afraid now. Go ahead if you don't want to come," Sasha said, and started to walk. Yang followed Sasha to an even smaller hotel at the end of a narrow lane. An old man was sitting behind a desk, playing poker with himself. "Grandpapa," Sasha said, handing her ID to the old man. "Do you have a single room for my brother and me?"

The old man looked at Sasha and then Yang. "He's not fifteen yet so he doesn't have an ID," Sasha said, and Yang smiled shyly at the old man, his white teeth flashing in the dark.

The old man nodded and handed a registration pad to Sasha. Five minutes later they were granted a key. It was a small room on the second floor, with two single beds, a rusty stand with two basins, and a window that did not have a curtain. Roaches scurried to find a hiding place when Sasha turned on the light. They stood just inside the door, and all of a sudden, she did not know what the excitement was of spending a night together in a filthy hotel. "Why don't we just go home?" Yang said behind her.

"Where's the place you call home?" Sasha snapped. She turned off the light and lay down on a bed without undressing. "Go back to the man who keeps you if this is not a place for a princess like you," she said.

Yang stood for a long moment before he got into the other bed. Sasha waited for him to speak, and when he did not, she became angry with him, and with herself.

The next morning, when the city stirred to life, they both lay awake in their own beds without talking. The homing pigeons flew across the sky, the small brass whistles bound to their tails humming in a harmonious, low tone. Not far away, Tao music played on a tape recorder, calling for the early risers to join the practice of tai chi. Old men, the fans of Peking Opera, sang their favorite parts of the Opera, their voices cracking at high notes. Then the doors down the lane creaked open, releasing the shouting children headed to school and adults to work, their bicycle bells clanking noisily.

Later, someone turned on a record player, and music blasted across the alley. Sasha sat up and looked out of the window. A young man was setting up a newspaper stand at the end of the alley, making theatrical movements along with a song in which a rock singer was yelling: *"Oh, Genghis Khan, Genghis Khan, he is a powerful old man. He is rich, he is strong, and I want to marry him.*"

Sasha listened to the song repeat and said, "I don't understand why these people think they have the right to trash Genghis Khan."

"Their ears are dead to real music," Yang said.

"When I was little, my father taught me a song about Genghis Khan. It was the only Mongolian song I remember now," Sasha said, and opened her mouth to sing the song. The melody was in her mind, but no words came to her tongue. She had forgotten almost all of the Mongolian words she had learned after her parents' divorce; she had not seen her father for fifteen years. "Well, I don't remember it anymore."

"*The broken pillars, the slanted roof,*" Yang chanted in a low voice, "*they once saw the banqueting days; the dying trees, the withering peonies, they once danced in the heavenly music. The young girls dreamed of their lovers who were enlisted to fight the Huns. They did not know the loved ones had become white bones glistening in the moonlight.*" Yang stared at the ceiling. "Our masters say that real arts never die. Real arts are about remembrance."

"What's the point of remembering the song, anyway?" Sasha asked. "I don't even remember what my father looked like." She thought about her father, one of the offspring of Genghis Khan. Genghis Khan was turned into a clown in the pop song. Mongolia was once the biggest empire in the world, and now it was a piece of meat, sandwiched by China and Russia.

"We live in a wrong time," Yang said.

Sasha turned to look at Yang. He lay on his hands and stared at the ceiling, his face taking on the resigned look of an old man. It hurt her, and scared her, too, to glimpse a world beneath his empty beauty. "We were born into a wrong place is what our problem is," she said, trying to cheer him and herself up. "Why don't you come to America with me, Yang?"

Yang smiled. "Who am I to follow you?"

"A husband, a lover, a brother, I don't care. Why don't you get out of Beijing and have a new life in America?" The words, once said, hung in the room like heavy fog, and Sasha wondered if Yang, too, had difficulty breathing. Outside the window, a vendor was sharpening a chopper with a whetstone, the strange sound making their mouths water unpleasantly. Then the vendor started to sing in a drawn-out voice about his tasty pig heads.

"Sasha," Yang said finally. "Is Sasha a Mongolian name?"

"Not really. It's Russian, a name of my mom's favorite heroine in a Soviet war novel."

"That's why it doesn't sound Chinese. I would rather it is a Mongolian name," Yang said. "Sasha, the princess of Mongolia."

Sasha walked barefoot to Yang's bed and knelt beside him. He did not move and let Sasha hold his face with both hands. "Come to America with me," she said. "We'll be the prince and the princess of Nebraska."

"I was not trained to play a prince," Yang said.

"The script is changed," Sasha said. "From today on."

Yang turned to look at Sasha. She tried to kiss him, but he pushed her away gently. *"A beautiful body is only a bag of bones,"* he sang in a low voice.

Sasha had never seen Yang perform, and could not imagine him onstage; he had played princesses and prostitutes, but he did not have to live with the painted mask and the silk costume. "The Peking Opera is dead," she said. "Why don't you give it up?"

"Who are you to say that about the Peking Opera?" Yang said.

Sasha saw the sudden iciness in Yang's eyes, and let the topic drop. Afterwards, neither mentioned anything about the stay in the hotel. A week later, when Boshen was escorted away from Beijing, Sasha was relieved and scared. There was, all of a sudden, time for them to fill. To her relief and disappointment, Yang seemed to have forgotten the moment when they were close, so close that they were almost in love.

The parade started with music and laughter, colorful floats moving by on which happy people waved to the happy audience. Boshen looked at Sasha's face lit up by curiosity, and sighed. Despite her willfulness and unfriendliness, the thought of the baby—Yang's baby—made him eager to forgive her. "Do you still not want to tell Yang about the baby?" he said.

"You've asked this the hundredth time," Sasha said. "Why should I?"

"He might want to come to America if he learned about the baby," Boshen said.

"There's no baby after tomorrow," Sasha said. She had tried Yang's phone number when she had learned of the pregnancy; she had tried his pager, too. At first it was measured by hours and days, and then it became weeks since she had left the message on his pager. He might have been living in another apartment with a new telephone number. The pager might no longer have belonged to him. She knew he had every reason for not getting her message, but she could not forgive his silence. In the meantime, her body changed. She felt the growth inside her, and she was disgusted by it. Sometimes she hated it from morning till night, hoping that it would finally go away somehow, surrendering to the strength of her resentment. Other times she kept her mind away for as long as she could, thinking that it would disappear as if it had never existed. Still, in the end, it required her action. In the end, it was just a chunk of flesh, and blood.

"But why was there a baby in the first place?" Boshen said. Why and how it happened were the questions that had been haunting him since he had heard from Sasha. He wanted to ask her if she, too, had been dazzled by the boy's body, smooth, lithe, perfectly shaped. He wanted to know if she had loved him as he had, but in that case, how could she have the heart to discard what had been left with her?

Sasha turned to Boshen. For the first time, she studied the man with curiosity. Not handsome nor ugly, he had a candid face that Sasha thought she could not fall in love with but nonetheless could trust. A man like Boshen should have had an ordinary life, boring and comfortable, yet his craze for Yang made him a more interesting man than he deserved to be. But that must have been what was Yang's value—he made people fall in love with him, and the love led them astray, willingly, from their otherwise tedious paths. Yang had been the one to bring up the idea of spending a night together again, and Sasha the one to ask a friend for the use of her rented room, a few days before Sasha's flight. It was one of the soggiest summer evenings. After their lovemaking, sweet and short and uneventful, they stayed on the floor, on top of the blanket Sasha had brought for the purpose, an arm's length in between them, each too warm to touch the other. Outside, the landlady's family and two other neighbor families were sitting in the courtyard and watching a TV program, their voices mixed with the claps of their hands killing the mosquitoes. Sasha turned to look at Yang, who was lying with his back to her. The little pack of condoms she had bought was tucked underneath the blanket, unopened. She had suggested it, and he had refused. A rubber was for people who touched without loving each other, Yang had said; his words had made her hopeful. "Do you want to come to America with me now?" she asked, tracing his back with one finger.

"What am I going to do in America? Be kept as a canary by you?" Yang said and moved farther away from her finger.

"You can spend some time learning English, and get a useful degree in America."

"Useful? Don't you already know that I am useless? Besides, nothing humiliates a man more than living as a parasite on his woman," Yang said, and reached for a silk robe he had packed with him. Before Sasha had the time to stop him, he walked out of the door. Sasha jumped to her feet and watched from behind the curtain; Yang walked with a calculated laziness, not looking at the people who turned their eyes away from the television to stare at him. When he reached the brick sink in the middle of the courtyard, he sat on the edge and raised his bare legs to the tap. The water had run for a long moment before the landlady recovered from her shock and said, "Hey, the water costs me money."

Yang smiled. "It's so hot," he said in a pleasant voice.

"Indeed," the landlady agreed.

Yang turned off the tap and walked back to the room with the same grace and idleness, knowing that the people in the courtyard were all watching him, his willowy body wrapped in the moon-white robe. Sasha stood by the window, cold with disappointment. She became his audience, one of the most difficult to capture, perhaps, but he succeeded after all.

A Disney float approached the corner where Sasha and Boshen stood. "Look," Sasha said and pointed at a giant glove of Mickey Mouse moving ahead of the float. "There're only four fingers."

"I didn't know that," Boshen said.

"Yang needs us no more than that glove needs us for our admiration," Sasha said.

"But our love is the only thing to protect him, and to save him, too."

Sasha turned and looked into Boshen's eyes. "It's people like us who have destroyed him, isn't it? Why was there *Nan Dan* in the Peking Opera in the first place? *Men loved him because he was playing a woman; women loved him because he was a man playing,*" she said.

"That's totally wrong."

"Why else do you want so much to put him back to the stage? Don't think I'm happy to see him fall. Believe me, I wanted to help him as much as you do. He didn't have to be a man playing a woman—I thought I would make him understand. But what did I end up with? You're not the one who has a baby inside; he's not the one having an abortion," Sasha said, and started to cry.

Boshen held out his hand hesitantly, touching Sasha's shoulder. If only she could love Yang one more time, Boshen thought. Yang could choose to live with either of them; he could choose not to love them at all, but their love would keep him safe and intact; they could—the three of them—bring up the baby together. Yang would remain the princess, exiled, yes, but a true princess, beautiful in a foreign land. If only he knew how to make Sasha love Yang again, Boshen thought.

Sasha did not move away when Boshen put an arm around her shoulder. They must look like the most ordinary couple to the strangers, she thought. A nervous husband comforting his moody wife after an argument. They might as well be a couple, out of love, he caring only for the baby inside her, she having no feeling left for anything, her unborn child included.

As if in responding, the baby moved. A tap, and then another one, gentle and tentative, the first greeting that Sasha had wished she would never have to answer, but it seemed impossible, once it happened, not to hope for more. Sasha held her breath and waited. After a long moment, people in the street shouted, and children screamed out of excitement. Sasha looked up—the lights were lit up in the trees, thousands of stars forming a constellation. She thought about the small Mongolian town where her mother lived alone now, her long shadow trailing behind her as she walked home along the dimly lit alley. Her mother had been born into a wrong time. Lived all her adult life in a wrong place. Yet she had never regretted the births of her two daughters. Sasha held her breath and waited for more of the baby's messages. America was a good country, she told herself, a right place to be born into. Everything was possible in America, and she imagined a baby possessing the beauty of her father but happier, and luckier. Sasha smiled, but when the baby moved again, she burst into tears. Being a mother must be the saddest yet most hopeful thing in the world, she thought—falling into a love that, once started, would never end.

MAXINE KUMIN

Where Any of Us

Where any of us is
going in tomorrow's reckless Lexus is
the elemental mystery: despite

instructions he left behind, Houdin-
i, who could outwit
ropes and chains, padlocks and steam-

er trunks, could extricate
himself from underwater metal crates,
could send forth, he was certain,

a message from the other side,
never cracked the curtain
and Mary Baker Eddy's telephone

said to be hooked up in her crypt—
would it have been
innocence or arrogance,

such trust in the beyond?—
has, mythic, failed to ring. If
they knew the script

these two (God may be love
or not) they left, tightlipped
and unfulfilled.

As we will.

Psalm 20

translated by Jennifer Grotz

When you appease my heart, I've nothing left to say,
my agitated words fall fast asleep.

I don't even remember my petty dramas—
your lullaby sings me awake.

Others assure me I imagine this, that to receive you
the wound in my chest must stay fresh.

And that the anguish of others reopens the cut,
and that it's not good to suppress their clamor.

It's not that they're wrong, you come to me this way, too,
but nothing compares to when you come to me like a dawn,

A brief dawning where everything is taken with adoration
of you, and then you go, you go to someone else's darkness.

The Passion of Saint Joseph

translated by José Edmundo Ocampo Reyes

> *No matter how much he pondered*
> *the Virgin's pregnancy, how much*
> *his thoughts went back and forth,*
> *his heart and troubled soul*
> *couldn't figure it out.*
> —traditional Filipino verse narrative of
> the life and death of Christ

Chisel, plane, and hammer,
to you I'll whisper
my bitter secret:
I haven't done it yet,
but my betrothed is already with child.

The angel tells me there's nothing
to be ashamed of,
no reason to weep;
in fact, I should rejoice,
for it was God Himself who raped her.

Hammer, plane, and chisel,
how does a carpenter cope
with his rage? Grin and bear it.
Faced with heaven, we lowly tradesmen
haven't a fighting chance!

Man go

The powerlessness of sleep to transport two men along a sand-blown road. The shrapnel keeps popping out of their bodies and the Humvee keeps crashing into the guardrail. The escarpment fills in with blood. The lieutenant rides shotgun, fallow with the land. He notices the flamingo thin stems of the frangipani, shredded in wind, unstitchable. He considers needlework, embroidery, all the dying arts, his foot soles stained orange, having hidden himself in the bush among the scattered stellae. Someone firing at him instead of opening her arms. He pictures her hieroglyphic, her constricted body hidden under bridge slats, then his own. He'd like to get his pulpy heart and go home, though he'd feel nostalgic for the men he's fought beside. Entrenched in such falconry, tunneling deep down, the wind licks at the tires, studs them with glass, stones, metal, and blood. A spider monkey jerks his head toward the road, scurries down the crumpling stone steps of a way-station temple, then screws himself into the grasp of the outstretched men.

Burn

That owl was an omen
Driving home from the airport
Not once but twice
It rose in my headlights
From rain black asphalt
Great white wings nearly touching
Windshield wipers   that low flying escort
Stretching sixty miles toward Alabama
The owl was always right
Something died and something else
Was just about to
I checked my daughter's red-eye slumber
In the rearview mirror
No need to worry her with divination
An hour drive delayed by rain
And now this trepidation on the slick black road
Certain as miscarried fortune
Her coming home to Mama in an autumn storm
And no such thing as California
Just a red clay creek bed down the road
From the house I birthed her in
Filling up to bathe away a sorrow
Blinking lights behind us
Before I hear the sirens
Fire truck passes on the narrow bridge
Then Crabtree Church in flames beyond the graveyard
My daughter wakes and guesses lightning
But I never heard the thunder crack
And only saw the lightning white of dreaded wings
I pull in   step out   and open an umbrella
Stand with the firemen   watch the frame fall down
The Marshall asks if we saw anything
Like kids driving away in a four-wheeler

They found tracks in the mud
Whiskey and beer bottles   a gas can
Burn! All those years of homecoming
Annual dinners on the grounds
Hymns around a weather-warped piano
Burn! My granddad's Indian education
Walls that heard a thousand lessons
A thousand prayers in high soprano
Burn! Fifty paper funeral parlor fans
Cokesbury hymnals and sixteen pews
Reduced to flaky carbon tamped with rain
The death of wood and glass
And half a baby's ashes in my daughter's pocketbook
All the little names we'll never sing
I aim to find that messenger again and scare him off
Litter the road with his insolent feathers

At Pine Ridge Pow Wow Grounds

Everything dies, baby, that's a fact, but maybe
everything that dies someday comes back.
—Bruce Springsteen

The bitter glue of snow makes the seven-hour trip take twelve.
I'm crying—have been sobbing off and on for more than two
days. I'm a pitiful, middle-aged mess. Goggles is in the trunk in a
Hefty Bag and Gizzard is snoring in Pekinese on the back seat.
The red devil of drink is on my left shoulder, jabbering, railing
against his cotton-mouthed banishment of twelve long years.

It's dusk when I hit the Rez and cruise into Pine Ridge Village. I
pull past the softball field named for Colleen's brother Delmar
and park at the pow wow grounds. Near a shabby stand of gaunt
ash, I lay Goggles down like she's some sweet, enchanted princess,
sleeping peacefully on a bed of new snow. In the time it takes to
smoke a Marlboro, she is nearly covered with white crystal glitter.
Corpulent tears, as bitter as I ever cried, waddle down my age-
cracked face. In the midst of such appalling sadness, I force out a
contemptuous snicker followed by a bone-rattling shudder. It's
either that or fall down dead myself.

Oh Goggles, you're home now. Sixteen years ago we stood in this
same exact spot and then you followed me into my mangy life. What
a flea-ridden, stinky, sad puppy you were. And what a crazed, wild
ride lay ahead of us. Sleep now. Sleep, little girl. When you wake in
the spring, you'll really run fast. Yeah, you'll really run lickety-split.
When you wake, the drummers will be drumming and the dusty
dusk of the wacipi *will intoxicate us. Muscular and contemptuous*
young hip-hop Skins will be swaggering, pints and joints stashed in
their back pockets. Your average NDNZ will be looking for hope like
pitifully poor people across the globe do. Sunka, you can stay for the
flag song, but then you must dance back home. Dance back through

my tart and loving memories. Dance past the blinding bitterness blazing in my brain.

I wipe the snow from her brow and kiss her nose. Then I drive away with Gizzard still snoring on the back seat of my senile Crown Victoria. The dirty streets of Pine Ridge carry me back to the squalor of my own youth. For an instant I'm young and the good red road ahead is not dead, nor filled with holes that can swallow the soul.

JEREDITH MERRIN

The Resistant Reader in the Age of Memoir: I

In her book, she said the guiding principle
was guarding against irreparable losses;
she'd managed to live so as

to avoid any major cause of regret.

Anyone who's done that, raise your hand:
you're excused from this poem.

As for us who remain, let's go around
the circle and list our regrets.
For the stuporous, self-evading hours.

For offhand, wounding sarcasms.

For narcissistic hatred of the imperfect
body that has hampered love.

For fatigued, five o'clock snapping
at the over-amped three-year-old.
For withholding, out of harbored

resentment, the wholehearted response.

For everyday, ape-in-hierarchy,
lies of assent . . .

But maybe she meant larger,
one-time-only things avoided?
The sale of the family house, say,

an abortion, the laceration of divorce?

But what servility was kept with that house,
what cowardice clung to with the brave

delivery of the baby, what fear of darkness
retained with the long-lasting marriage?
(And is there a word for the regret

of having too few regrets?

Oh, there must be—in French?)
Remember that adolescent moment, poised

before first sex—with already,
how many regrets? Who knows the number
of planets where life might start over?

On one, an ocean with a new tide. Trees, maybe?

So beautiful. They grow and fall in one place,
never experiencing irreparable loss.

Schumann, Op. 16: The Greater Happiness

On the stage Robert Schumann is getting drunk

With tempestuous love. You remember what it is to listen to
    passionate
Nineteenth-century music, a clamor of argument and struggle
Invoking the old gods, thunderbolt and hurricane,
At the moment of their dying, and here in the lightning
Is Clara whose father forbids her to marry him.

The middle-aged pianist plunges through the keys.

I sit back, enjoy the performance, then suddenly find myself
Inside a glissando as inside a storm, flooded and windswept,
Then sense on my face an expression of my shy dead father's,
A twitch of ironic rue at the eyebrow, and presently I feel him
Look through my eyes like sea-cave openings, bone binoculars.

The pianist pours his strength into Robert's ferocity.
Somewhere under the hurricane a sea turtle rows through
    silence.

Thunder sings, fleecy skies shine, and my father can see
The music through my skull's apertures. He is happy for me
That in my life I can wallow in such music, not like his life.
Our family didn't do beauty, we did poverty, his soul aches with
    regret.
He, too, might have loved beauty but whatever you miss in this
    life you miss forever.

We sit together, my face awash in tears, pity for his jocular
    sneakers, his union card,
His eyes jealous when I went to college, my mother's pointless
    tirades,

My useless guilt. A girl who helplessly watches her tigress mother
Harass her mousy father year after year must crave escape, but
    the truth
Is I abandoned him. So I praise God

That the roads between the worlds are open again,
Then he says to my soul, not in words, *Tell your mother I love her.*
And my soul is still more happy sitting in the velvet seat in the
    front orchestra
Following the cadenza like an engine of tears, like a wet silence,
    arpeggios
Trembling in every direction, *He loves her, he always loved her,*
    the wave

That overwhelms us is only a portion of ocean, what flooded my
    parents was just
Thirty years of tragic human love, like between Robert and
    Clara,
Like all passion when the gods are still alive,
And somewhere under the hurricane a sea turtle rows through
    silence,
Somewhere my father rocks asleep on the wave.

ELISE PASCHEN

Engagement

The king is murdered and his daughter, Mis, goes mad,
growing fur and killer claws, escaping into the woods.
She is tamed by Dubh Ruis, a harp player.
Marrying her, he becomes king.
                        —Irish legend

Don't touch me, don't come near. I'll shred
your flesh from bone. Don't even stare.

I can smell you from here. You don't
reek like the hunters who tailed me,

all salt and sod. You smack of hay.
Show me what you're hiding. The strings

trap a sun's glint. Sounds like leaf-play
at night beneath a tree. Here's where

I lay me down—inside this notch.
Play it for me and let me play.

                        *

What's in your mouth? You swallow hard.
It's coming back. A waking whiff—

out on the flagstones in the courtyard,
through the doorways, the gates.

I feel I'm coming home. It's like
a hearth. I never get enough.

                        *

Nights I still rave. The beast is out.
Your arms around me pin it down.

*

Your collar's tight. But look. My fingers
have grown shells now, not claws. Stop tying

that cloth across my skin. I need
the air, these woods. Keep here. Let's stay

above moss, beneath leaf. Help me
shake down rowans, rub our flesh red.

You've stripped away the fur, and, after
months of those deer-fat baths, I'm bare.

Bert Wilson Plays Jim Pepper's
Witchi-Tai-To at the Midnight Sun

Don't look up, because the ceiling is suffering
some serious violations of the electrical code,
the whole chaotic kelplike mess
about to shower us with flames.
I think I can render this clearly enough—

Bert's saxophone resting between his knees
and propped against the wheelchair's seat
where his body keeps shape-shifting—
he's Buddha then Shop-Vac then Buddha again,
formlessness floating on top of form.

The problem is back-story, how to get it all in,
not just Bert's beanie and tie-dye T-shirt
but polio, too, and the tune itself, concentric ripples
widening. So now dead Jim Pepper
comes floating in, and next comes his grandfather,

fancy-dancing and chanting. How to tender
the lead-in, would phonemes do any good—
(the signature *DAHH*, the *doon doons* down-marching)
or just call it a prayer to simplify things
as Bert bends the melody's slim reed

way past the point where it should break?
Then he puts the mouthpiece aside
to bring up the words from the floor of his soul
or say from the pads of his spud-shaped feet
spraddling the footplate, if *soul* is too hokey

for all the misty goo inside us.
First comes the Creek part of the song
and then comes the English, when Bert throws back his chin:
his underbeard raised in a coyote salute
to the water infusing the warehouse roof.

Here, take a seat on these rickety risers
inside my head, though your life isn't mine,
still I have hope for your hearing
the gist of this refrain
about how glad he is that he's not dead.

DAVID ROMTVEDT

Once Strangers on a Train

When the poles clatter past,
the years fall away, a spider drops
from the petals of a flower, space
is ever more empty the larger it grows,
the steel wheels chunk-chunk-chunk
on the joints of the rails, the friction
making sparks, stars crushed
and invisible to us inside.

There is a distance that diminishes
as the point of departure recedes.
I fall asleep and my head drops
onto your shoulder. You let me
rest there so that when I awake
I can smell your foreign skin and feel
the wet spot on your blouse, my mouth open.

I hold you in my arms again,
harder than I did that first time,
harder than the glass holding us
inside the compartment, our bodies
inside our skin. I am only and forever
that man and you, that woman.

I whispered some word
and you held your hand up, shushed me.
We could hear a traveler turn in the dark,
uncomfortable, a slight groan or sigh,
all of us third-class passengers, our souls
sleeping on hard benches.

When you drop your hand to my lap,
I realize our lips are so close.
I feel your breath, then touch.
Where are we?
Where are the swallows
who bank and turn as we enter the tunnel?
The dust that rises as we pass?
The lips? And again, the kiss.

Santorini: Fragmentos

Braced against the worst gusts yet this summer
astride the promontory's highest ridge,
           breathless
we stare out across sea-glare
                into distance
diaphanous as mist.

*

Wind-whirred grass buzzes our ankles here
where temples rise bone-bright through
blood worship with a view.
                  The present
scatters roughly like whitecaps on a sea-face.

*

We can't help but know our local queries
echo off toward sky like light from fire,
                          nor
would we want grass turning into tongues
or stones nudging up through earth to crack
their gritty lips and speak, decanting mysteries.

*

Blood can sanctify intention with its
blessing, but this was not our blood,
and these were not our purposes.

*

                              We're
here as careless innocents,
awkward in the wreckage of such
stiff-necked heroics, cameras dangling
from our sweaty throats.

*

                              Silenced
we gawk, surrounded by potent images
whose presence in our lenses
and absence in our hearts
conspire to blind us.

*

                              And we are
stripped of guile. The path
that brought us here
can take us down again, grateful
for having found a way back
to the commonplace.

*

                              In our bones
we know this place is holy.

*

                              In our hearts
we don't know what that means.

JESS ROW

The Train to Lo Wu

Whenever I remember Lin, I think of taxicabs. We spent so much of our time sitting in the back of one, somewhere in Shenzhen—speeding away from the border-crossing station, or returning to it. In my memory it was always a bright morning, sun streaming through the dusty windows, or late at night, our bodies striped with the colors of the neon lights passing overhead. We sat on opposite sides of the seat, our hands folded, like brother and sister; she wouldn't let me speak, or even touch her leg. If the driver heard my terrible Mandarin, she said, he and his friends would know exactly who she was: another country girl peddling herself to a Hong Kong man for easy money.

I obeyed her, of course. And that's why I was so surprised the one time she broke her own rule. We had just turned the corner at the Kuroda hotel; we were five minutes away from Lo Wu, the border crossing to Hong Kong. She turned to me and said, If I don't call you this week, what will you do?

I'll call you, of course. Why do you ask?

No. That's not what I mean. What if I never called you again?

She had put on a new shade of lipstick that morning, one I had bought for her; against her skin it looked like fresh blood. It made me shiver.

Then I would come and find you. One way or another.

But you couldn't, she said. If you never called *me*, I could find your number in the Hong Kong directory. I could find your family and where you worked. But what could you do? China is too big. If I disappear, that's it. China will swallow me up.

She was right about the driver: he turned his head towards us as he drove, to hear better, and when we came to a traffic light he turned and gave me a salacious grin. I wanted to curse at him. But all the curses I know are Cantonese, and he wouldn't have understood.

Lin, what do you want me to say? I said. You're right, of course. If you *want* to disappear, you can. One way or the other, it's in your power.

Her eyes widened, as if my answer had made her suddenly angry. What makes you so sure of that? she said. What makes you so confident?

I didn't know what to say. We were pulling into the long line of taxis in front of the station; the street was filled with people hurrying towards the entrance. My legs itched. *I'll see you next week,* I wanted to say, but I knew, without wanting to know, that the words didn't matter. The driver turned around in his seat and looked from my face to hers, eager to hear the last line. I took out a wad of hundred-yuan bills and gave him the dirtiest one.

When you get on the train, she said, it's like a dream, isn't it? As if none of this ever really happened. That's good. You should keep it that way. Sometimes dreams happen over and over again, sometimes they don't.

Lin, I said, that's the most ridiculous—

She opened the door and strode away quickly, pushing through the crowd, like a fish, fighting its way upstream.

If it were not for Little Brother, I would never have thought about China. I live in the New Territories, not far from the border, and the train to Lo Wu passes through the station I use every day, but I had never once considered taking it there. I don't have any relatives in China—my family has lived in Hong Kong for five generations—and I don't like to travel. I've never had that kind of curiosity. And I suppose I still remember the stories my parents' friends told, about the Communists and the Second World War—stories that gave me nightmares as a child. Rows of bodies and babies impaled on bayonets. You could say that for me China was a place that only existed in the past, but not *my* past, a memory that wasn't mine to have.

My own life is really very simple. My parents died years ago, when I was in college; I was an only child, and they left me a portfolio of real estate holdings, and their apartment in Tai Wo. During the day I manage the accounts at an oil trader in Kwai Hing, and in the afternoon, every afternoon, I take the bus to the Shek O Sailboard Club, at the far southeastern tip of Hong Kong Island. If you've ever taken a ferry or a junk trip around the island, you've probably seen me in the distance, crossing your path: a tiny, dark figure attached to a bright triangle of sail, hurtling across the waves like a pebble from a slingshot. This is Big Wave Bay, where the typhoons come ashore, where the world speed record was once set. My nickname is *fei yu,* flying fish, and it's true. Two days out of the water is a lifetime to me.

It'll take two hours, Little Brother told us one Friday night, in the back room of the Sha Tin Bar. Cross the border, change some money, take a taxi, pick up some boxes, and go back home. What could be easier than that?

We looked at him skeptically. Little Brother is the youngest of five friends I've had since primary school—the Five Brothers, we call ourselves—and like a real little brother, he's the wild one: he dyed his hair blond and started racing motorcycles in Form Three, when he was only fourteen. Now he owns his own repair shop in Mong Kok and takes his grandmother to play mah jongg every Sunday.

What's in the boxes? Siu Wong asked him.

Parts. Honda parts.

Are they stolen?

How should I know? All I heard is that they're there. Half the price I pay for them to come from Japan.

Why do you need all five of us? I asked.

You never know what's going to happen, he said. It's Shenzhen, isn't it? And I thought we might explore a little bit, since we're there. You know, Hong Kong people live like kings in China. The best of everything. He winked.

I hesitated: it wasn't my idea of a good way to spend a Sunday afternoon in April. But if he wanted my help, how could I refuse? It sounded so easy—all I had to do was bring my passport.

None of the five of us are married. I should have mentioned that.

When you step out of the border-crossing into Shenzhen, at first it seems that the air is full of dust, but actually it's the pollution that gives the light a milky quality, even on the clearest of days. Everything seems oversized: wide, empty sidewalks, and six-lane avenues, a train station that stretches across four city blocks, skyscrapers whose tops disappear in the haze. Even the policemen's uniforms are baggy and loose, as if they were children playing dress-up in their parents' clothes. All around you are things for sale—Nikes, North Face jackets, Tissot watches, new movies on VCD—and only when you move closer can you see the badly photocopied labels peeling off, the zippers hanging loose, the image blurred on the package. If you stop anywhere for too long, somebody will push you from behind and snap a few harsh syllables you recognize, but only barely. I studied Mandarin in school, and speak it quite well, but still I always remember what my mother used to say, that she could never trust anyone whose voice reminded her of a squeaking rodent, a rat caught in a trap.

All through that first taxi ride I kept my face close to the window, ignoring the conversation, trying to absorb everything I saw. Buildings made of white tile, the kind used for bathrooms, with windows of blue-tinted glass; a woman in a soldier's uniform riding a bicycle, her daughter balanced precariously on the crossbar; a man in an ill-fitting suit and loafers, shoveling coal into a wicker basket. Little Brother standing on a sidewalk, smoking cigarette after cigarette, and arguing with the shop owner in fractured Cantonese. It did no good: all the parts had already been sold. I remember looking at my watch and realizing that four hours had already gone by, and thinking that when we arrived back at the border it would feel as if no time had passed at all.

I tell you what, Little Brother said at some point. Let's not make this trip a total failure. I'll take you guys to Club Nikko. It's in the Radisson—we can walk to the border from there.

There's a Radisson here?

Of course, he said impatiently. This is Shenzhen. They have everything.

Later I used to tease Lin about how she looked, the first time we met: dressed in a white and baby-blue miniskirt, knee-high boots, and a Löwenbräu hat, a living commercial. She was a bargirl, who swooped down on tables before the waitress arrived, gave out free lighters and coasters, and offered Löwenbräu at a "special price," and she was terrible at it. Her voice was high-pitched and squeaked with nervousness, and she mangled the Cantonese tones; the customers' laughter sent her bouncing from table to table like a pinball. Little Brother was telling a long story about the first time he visited the Guangzhou racetrack, and eventually I lost the thread of it, and leaned back from the table. By that time it was late, and no new customers were coming in; she was standing against the wall in back, by the bathroom door, and even across that darkened room I could see her cheeks burning.

Going to the toilet, I said, setting down my beer. Siu Wong, sitting next to me, slapped me on the back. As I passed I glanced at her, and she looked away; tracks of mascara were beginning to run from the corners of her eyes.

Here, take this, I said abruptly, taking a packet of Kleenex from my jacket and thrusting it at her. She accepted it silently. I went into the bathroom, used the toilet, and washed my hands several times over. When I looked into the mirror, my own face was red.

Thanks, she said, as soon as I opened the door, and handed me back the packet of tissues. Where she had wiped around her eyes was now blue-black, and she looked like a panda bear. I feel better now. Everything's okay.

It's not your fault, I said, awkwardly, trying to remember the Mandarin words. It isn't your language. Maybe next time try a bar without so many Hong Kong people.

Hong Kong people *tip*.

I must have looked bewildered, because she laughed in my face, with a harsh sound. Ai ya, she said, you really are one of them, aren't you? Haven't you ever been to China before?

Never.

Well, let me tell you something you don't know. I have a college degree. You won't catch me working in some bar for lowlifes. This is good money.

What was your degree?

Primary school education.

She crossed her arms and turned her head away, glancing at me sideways. *She's waiting for me to laugh,* I realized, and pursed my lips and nodded, as if it were the most normal thing in the world. You couldn't find a teaching job here? I asked.

Are you crazy? A country girl like me, from Anhui?

Maybe I can help. I took a business card from my wallet and gave it to her, and she accepted it formally, with both hands. I have some friends who work in Shenzhen, I said. Maybe they could find you something better. Have you ever worked as a secretary?

She wasn't listening; she was still reading the card, her lips moving silently. *Hah vay,* she said. That's your name?

It's pronounced *Harvey.*

Well, listen, Harvey, she said, turning to face me, her arms still crossed. I won't embarrass you by giving your card back in front of your friends, but I'm not interested in your kind of help.

But I was just—

Are you deaf? Leave me alone!

When I returned to the table, Little Brother had already told them the punchline, and everyone was reeling with laughter, clinking their bottles for another round. Siu Wong leaned over to my ear.

You can do much better than that, he said. Why play around in the trash? Just ask Little Brother to take you to Second Wives Village sometime.

It was all I could do not to turn and smack him across the face.

I don't think I was as naïve as I must have seemed to her that day. I knew how many men go over the border on "business trips," and how many Chinese women stay in Shenzhen for years, waiting to be allowed into Hong Kong to join men they think are their husbands. But I'm not the kind of person to connect a face with something I saw on the TV news. And I'd never imagined that someone could look at me that way: as a predator, a slippery eel, as Hong Kong people say. For weeks I thought about her, rewording our conversation over and over, wondering if I could have done anything differently.

I was out sailing the first time she called. When I returned to my locker and checked my pager there was a strange, garbled message: *Club Nikko girl returning best time before 20:00,* and a Shenzhen telephone number. When I called, I could barely hear her voice over the blaring music and strange banging sounds in the background.

Where are you?

Never mind, she said. I want to meet you again. I'll be in the lobby of the Shangri-La at four on Friday.

I thought you would throw away the card. After what you said.

I think I might have made a mistake, she said. Did I?

Of course you did.

Just so you know, she said, I don't expect anything from you. And you shouldn't, either. We're starting off equal.

What do you mean?

You'll see, she said. See you there. And she hung up.

I'd only been to the Shangri-La in Hong Kong once, for an awards ceremony, but as I remembered it, the one in Shenzhen was an exact copy: chandeliers, marble, lots of mirrors, and thick carpet that swallowed the sound of your footsteps. Fancy hotels make me nervous; I always avoid them if I can. Being in one of those places makes me feel like someone has handed me something fragile—a glass bowl, an antique vase—and won't let me put it down.

She was waiting for me at a low table in the lobby, drinking coffee. I'd wondered if I would recognize her again, without the clothes, but even through the outside windows I picked her out immediately. Her hair was piled into a tight bun, and she was wearing a dark green jacket; even without the makeup her skin was as white as chalk. Nothing she did suggested she was waiting for someone. Her eyes rested on the floor; she brought the cup to her lips slowly, as if she had hours to finish it. I'd never met anyone so beautiful in that way, so severe and composed and self-contained.

When I walked up to her, she barely smiled.

I'm sorry about the phone call, she said. It was a bad line. I couldn't talk long.

It's all right. As soon as I sat down, a waiter appeared. Coffee, I said. What she's having.

Did it take you long to get here?

No. My apartment is only half an hour from the border. In Tai Wo.

She nodded politely. *She has no idea where that is,* I thought. *Don't be rude.* I feel awkward about this, I said. I don't even know your name.

Bai Ming is my name, she said. But everyone calls me Lin.

Like Lin in the book, right?

She gave me a puzzled look and shook her head.

Lin Dai-yu, I said. From *Dream of the Red Chamber*?

Lin was my elder sister, she whispered. She died when I was twelve.

I took a sip of coffee and looked around the lobby; in various mirrors I could see ten different reflections of our two heads, together, from a distance. As if we were man and wife, or brother and sister, or a boss and his secretary; as if there were one good reason for us to be sitting at the same table.

I didn't mean to embarrass you, I said. Maybe we should speak plainly. I'm not sure I understand why you asked me to come here. Did you want to find out about a job?

I wanted to talk, she said. I've never met anyone from Hong Kong before—just an ordinary person, I mean. I thought maybe that's what you were.

What do you mean by ordinary?

A person who doesn't want something.

I don't think I qualify for that, I said. Everybody wants *something*. It just happens that I don't come to China looking for it.

She stared at me for so long I shifted in my chair.

What is it that you want?

I shrugged. The same as everybody, I guess. Good fortune. More money. An apartment on the beach. A car. Good health. A family of my own.

You aren't married?

Does that surprise you? Do I seem married?

No, she said. I didn't think so. But where I come from you would *have* to be married.

I smiled. My parents are dead, I said. So no one's banging on my door asking for grandsons.

She looked down at her hands. Close-up her skin seemed thin and almost transparent, like rice paper; there were faint bluish shadows underneath her cheekbones. *Does she not eat?* I wondered. *Or not go out in the sun?*

So now we know one another's secrets, I said, and laughed, or tried to; it sounded more like coughing. That's a good way to begin, isn't it? We can't make any worse fools of ourselves.

You can leave, she said quickly. If you want to. Don't feel obligated to stay.

Not at all, I said. But I have a question for you. Why did you want to meet here? Isn't there someplace less formal?

I come here all the time, she said. It's quiet. It's clean. And there's all these chairs that hardly anyone ever sits in. The waiters all know me—I used to work in the bar downstairs. They don't care if I sit here for hours.

It seems very lonely to me.

That depends on how you look at it. I think it's peaceful.

I put down my cup and studied her face, as if for the first time. To me the word *peace*, the word *ningjing*, has a very specific, private meaning: it means the sound of the sea, of waves slapping against the board underneath me, and the feeling of crossing the bay on a stormy day when no other boats are out, and the water is the color of slate, and I'm all alone underneath a ceiling of clouds. Hong Kong people don't use this word very often, and when they do, you get the feeling they don't know what they're talking about.

I suppose you spend all of your free time in karaoke bars, she said.

No, I said. That's what I was just thinking about. It's exactly the opposite. Do you know what windsurfing is? She shook her head. I'll show you, I said, reaching for a napkin. Do you have a pen?

So I drew her a picture of a sailboard, and explained a little bit of how it's done, the way you stand and hold the boom and tilt the sail to turn, the way you feel the wind's changes on your shoulders and calves and the back of your head. While I was talking, her eyes began to flash a little, and she started asking questions. Why don't you fall over? What do you do if the wind dies? She laughed and shook her head with exasperation, as if she couldn't quite believe my answers. By that time it was almost five, and we both had to leave; when she asked me if I wanted to meet again I said yes, automatically, and then thought, *This is the first thing that has happened in my life that I could never explain to anyone.*

For the next month we met once every week, on Saturday afternoons, always at the Shangri-La. Once afterwards we went down the street to a Shanghai restaurant and ate lion's-head meatballs and Shaoxing pork. I always asked for the check; outside, so as not to embarrass me, she paid me for her half, in old two-yuan bills so soft they fell through my fingers and fluttered to the sidewalk. When I protested, the crinkles of laughter disappeared from the corners of her eyes, and she gave me a cold smile. If you want to see me, she said, you'll let me pay my share.

But it's ridiculous, I said. They won't even take these at the exchange window, do you know that?

She stooped and picked up the bills, bending her knees to one side, and stuffed them into my vest pocket. Keep them as a souvenir, she said. They're not so little to me.

I laughed, but I was the only one.

I would be the first to admit I'm no expert on love. Before Lin, I'd had other girlfriends, but really only by accident, and never for longer than a few months. A secretary in another division of my company, after we met at an office party. A friend of Siu Wong's little sister, who asked me to help her with some accounting problems. Every one of these relationships ended with some variation of the same phrase: *You're a nice man, but I don't think this should go any further. This isn't love.* And it was true, of course: I didn't feel anything special for any of them, not even during sex, not even at the moment of orgasm. The whole performance to me was so physical, so lacking in personal feeling, that I always felt a little embarrassed afterward and wished she would simply leave. After a few encounters this embarrassment became so strong that I couldn't even hold a conversation, and so it ended, quickly and quietly, with little protest from either of us.

There was a time in my mid-twenties when I wondered if I was gay, or asexual, if I would be happier as a lifelong celibate or a monk. I even considered going to a psychologist to see if there was something hidden in my past keeping me from being able to love. But I never went through with it. The sad truth is that it didn't bother me all that much. I had my friends; I had my health and strength; and I had the ocean, the waves and the wind—the one deep love of my life, you could say. You might say I decided to let fate choose for me. Probably, I thought, I *would* wind up married, and a father. But not by my own efforts, not by forcing the matter.

I never once considered the danger of this kind of passivity. I never thought that love would come out of the sky when I least expected it, like a storm on a clear day, and that I would have no choice but to bow down and face it, unprepared.

In all that time I never mentioned Lin to anyone. When my friends at the club asked where I was on Saturdays, I told them I was busy with an extra project at work; if Siu Wong called, I said I was too tired to go out. It wasn't simply a matter of embarrassment.

Every time I imagined what I would say—*She's very nice, smart, she has a college degree, she's really a teacher*—my stomach rolled up into a tight little ball. *Even so,* I heard Siu Wong saying, *what are you going to do next, live in Shenzhen? She doesn't have any connections—she can't leave. Do you think you can just become Chinese?*

That was the real question, of course. In Lin's eyes I was a nice man who wore track suits all the time and made silly jokes in bad Mandarin: all the rest of it, my parents, my job, my friends, were to her like shadows in a puppet show. And to me she was even more perplexing. Her parents were engineers who worked in a state-owned garment factory that made uniforms for the army. During the Cultural Revolution they were sent to the far west, to Gansu, and worked digging stones in a quarry; she was born there, in a mud hut with no running water. What could I ever say about that? All I knew about the Cultural Revolution was from movies.

In the end I did the only thing I could think of: I brought her the first volume of *Dream of the Red Chamber*. In the book Lin Dai-yu is the hero's true love, a beautiful, ethereal orphan whom he is forbidden to marry, because of her poor and inauspicious background. Eventually he is convinced to marry her rival, and she falls ill and dies of grief, but that was irrelevant to me; the first part of the novel is filled with the hero's dreams of her, and poems written in her honor. I gave it to her on a Saturday in March, and the next week it was sitting on the table by her elbow, wrinkled and dog-eared, when I came in.

Have you finished it already?

Finished it? Her eyes were puffy, I noticed, as if she hadn't slept, and hadn't bothered with makeup. I read it twice, she said. I think I don't understand you.

Didn't you like it?

Harvey, she said, she's an *orphan.* She lives far away from her hometown and she knows she'll probably never see the South again. All around her there are fabulously rich people, but she has no money of her own. How did you think it would make me feel?

It's a novel, I said. Not an essay on society. It's a love story.

She pushed it across the table, and it fell into my lap. Keep your novels, she said. I have enough problems.

I turned it over in my hands: the lamination peeling from the cover, the spine folded and broken. Lin, I said, tell me what you want.

She gave me a suspicious look. You mean right now?

In the future. Tell me what you want the most.

She stared down at her hands.

Or else I don't know why I should keep coming here, I said. What good are we to each other? You seem to think that I can't understand you, no matter how hard I try.

It's ridiculous, she said. You'll laugh at me.

The waiter brought our cups of coffee; I took a sip immediately, and burned my tongue. Go on, I said, wincing.

I want to have a kindergarten. She bit down on her lower lip, scraping it with her teeth. Not work in one. I've done that. I want to have a private kindergarten, like they do in Shanghai and Beijing, where the parents pay. That way you can have enough blankets and cots and chairs for every student. You can do painting and music and teach English. And you can get your own cook and have decent food. Only a certain number of students admitted every year.

There's nothing ridiculous about that, I said. How much would it cost?

She looked down at the table, a flush rising from her neck.

It's impossible. They wouldn't let me change my residency. And I would have to buy a new teacher's permit—if they would even sell me one.

Are you sure of that? I wanted to ask, but something stopped me—the way her shoulders seemed to go limp, or the bright spots on her cheeks. Thank you, I said. I'm glad you told me that.

Why?

Because I don't want to leave you.

She furrowed her eyebrows; for a moment I thought she hadn't understood me.

We can't talk this way. You don't know what you're saying.

I think we have to, I said. I don't think we can go on this way much longer.

You don't understand, she said. There's no other way. There aren't *options.*

Maybe we should go someplace where we can talk alone.

I live in a dormitory, she said. It's a women-only building. If anyone saw me with you I would be evicted overnight.

Then maybe we should—

Go to a hotel room?

I don't want to be vulgar, I said. I just want to spend more time with you.

There are places, she said, pressing her lips into a line. But you have to pay by the hour. And sometimes they don't clean the sheets in between.

Fine. Then I'll spend the night in a hotel, and we'll go out together for dim sum in the morning.

She shook her head. Understand this, she said. It isn't that I don't want to. But in Shenzhen, if you pretend to be a whore, you are a whore. And I won't do that. Not even for a second.

You don't have to, I said, tightening my fists under the table. It won't come to that.

It took me two weeks to find a solution. When I first told Little Brother what I wanted, he laughed so hard I took the phone away from my ear, and shouted at him to be quiet and get serious. Two days later, he faxed me a list of flats in Shenzhen that could be rented by the night, the week, or the month, no names taken, and no questions asked.

Don't you have any friends in Shenzhen? I asked him the next day. I'm looking for a—a more personal arrangement.

What does that mean?

I don't want to pay, I said. Not directly. Maybe you could give him a gift, and then I could reimburse you. But I don't want to have to give money directly. I made a promise.

You are a strange one, he said. What kind of girl is this?

She's very principled.

And you're going behind her back?

There's no other way. I'm not happy about it.

Whatever you say, flying fish, he said. All that salt water finally went to your head. I'll find you something.

When I told Lin about it, at first she refused. You're missing the point, she said. I told you already. If you pay for this, you might as well pay for everything. I won't belong to anyone, don't you see?

I'm not paying anyone anything, I said. Someone's doing me a favor. There's no money involved.

But it's *yours*. It's your friend. It's your power to say yes or no.

Then you decide, I said. I'll be there on Saturday. You can come or not.

That was how I came to stay at the apartment on Nanhai Lu. It was in a new building, painted white, at the end of a little strip of land that jutted into Shenzhen Bay. The rest of the strip was taken up by a hotel development that had been abandoned, leaving only concrete foundations and rusted metal prongs jutting into the sky. The apartment was on the fourth floor, and the bedroom windows faced the water; there were times when I woke up there and gazed out across the bay, forgetting where I was.

Sometimes Lin came on Saturday afternoons, left in the evening for work, and didn't return; but most weekends she came briefly on Saturday and all day Sunday. I took things as slowly as I knew how: we watched movies on the VCD player, played guess-fingers and Go, and listened to our favorite CDs, Chopin and Faye Wong and Kenny G. She taught me how to steam a whole fish with sweet wine sauce; I made her macaroni with ham and milk tea.

It sounds ridiculous to say so—especially now—but I think of those days as some of the happiest of my life. When the door closed, Lin became a different person. She took long showers, filling the apartment with steam, and came out of the bathroom barefoot, wearing a Polo sweatsuit I had bought for her at the border. The apartment had a set of two plastic-covered couches in the living room; she liked to lie back on one and prop her legs up on the other with her eyes closed. This reminds me of home, she said. Room to stretch out. No one watching you all the time.

Take off the plastic, I told her once. The landlord won't mind. It's supposed to come off.

Plastic is fine. She slapped the cushion for emphasis. It's *clean*. It doesn't get wet. It doesn't mildew.

But it's uncomfortable. Your legs stick to it.

Don't worry, she said softly, almost whispering. She was drifting off, as she often did; some Sundays she would nap for two hours in the middle of the morning. You know, Harvey, she said, her voice wavering with sleepiness, you're too kind. You're too good a person for this world. You should be more sensible.

I'm not so kind to everyone, I said. Only to you.

That's what I mean. I'm not such a wonderful person. I don't deserve it.

I don't believe that.

Do you know how I got to Shenzhen? She sat up, wiping her mouth on her sleeve, and curled her legs under her. Have I ever told you this story?

No.

I bribed a transit commissioner in Zhengzhou, she said. To get a residence permit. He wanted two cases of Marlboros and a bottle of Suntory whiskey. I got fake cigarettes from a guy I knew in my college. The whiskey was the hard part. I had to save up for six months to get one small bottle.

It's an unfair system. Why should you feel bad about that?

Not about that, she said. He was a huge, fat man, you know, so fat he could hardly fit behind his desk. His head looked like a balloon, it was perfectly round. And he had a mustache that only grew black on one side. When I gave him the cigarettes he opened the carton and started smoking one after another, at the same time he was filling out my form. He left these oily fingerprints all over it. And then, two weeks later, I heard he had a heart attack. Just fell over at his desk. And when I heard about it, I just started to laugh. I could see it so clearly. He was sucking those cigarettes so hard I thought he might keel over when I was there.

She giggled a little, and covered her mouth, but not so much that I couldn't see her broad smile. You see? she said. Do I deserve your kindness, Harvey? A man dies and all I can do is laugh.

Lin, I said, I don't blame you. If I were in your place I would have felt the same way.

But you weren't, she said. You've never had to do anything like that. Why should you have to sympathize with me? I've never been able to understand that. I'm not so special. Why do you have to go to all this trouble?

Maybe because you don't want me to, I said. I had meant it to be playful, but as soon as the words came out of my mouth, I realized it was the truth. You've had so much unhappiness in your life, I said. I don't blame you for doubting me. But I *want* to understand. Doesn't that count for something?

She shook her head. You can't, she said. It's pointless to try. It's masochistic. You know that, don't you?

Tell me to leave, if you want, I said. I felt suddenly angry; all the warmth had drained out of her face in an instant, as if she had willed it to. We're not as different as you think, I said. My parents are gone. I know what it's like to wake up and not know whether I'd rather be dead or alive. Don't tell me that just because I have money I've never suffered.

Stay, she said. She reached up and motioned for me to come to her. I sat down on the couch, and she leaned over and rested her head carefully on my shoulder. Let's not talk, she said. Talking just reminds me that I have to leave.

But otherwise we'll just be strangers.

We're strangers anyway, I expected her to say. She put her hand on my elbow, as if to keep me there. In a few minutes I heard her slow, steady breathing, and realized she was asleep.

Each time she came we kissed only once, just before she left, and over the weeks the kisses became longer and longer, until she dropped her bag of work clothes and stood in the doorway with her arms around my shoulders, tears starting in her eyes.

You don't have to go, I said. Tell them you were sick.

I'm supposed to be saving money, she said. Instead I'm spending it. If I don't show up they'll fire me then and there. In Shenzhen you don't get second chances.

You can find something better, I said. You're spending everything you make on taxis. It doesn't make any sense, Lin.

I told you. I warned you that it wouldn't work.

Let me help you, then.

She pressed a finger to my lips.

My life is so little to you, she whispered. A snap of the fingers. I'm the dust you shake off your shoes.

Do you think that's what I meant?

She shook her head. You don't have to mean it, she said. It just *is.*

It was June. In the evenings after she left, I went for walks along the concrete seawall that overlooked the bay, watching the sun melt through layers of haze. The water there was clotted with sewage and the shiny bellies of fish; without wanting to, I imagined myself paddling through it on top of my sailboard, and felt a shiver of nausea and disgust. *That isn't fair,* I thought. *There's always garbage on the beach at Shek O.* I turned to the east and looked up at the skyline, or what little of it I could see through the smog: a jumble of tall spires and cylinders and shining glass tower blocks, some of them copies of buildings in Hong Kong, others probably copied from buildings elsewhere in the world. *Why is it that Shenzhen doesn't look quite right?* I wondered. *Why does it seem like such a mirage, as if I might come back next week and find it gone?*

We slept together for the first time on the night of July 1, the first anniversary of the handover, of Hong Kong returning to China. From Nanhai Lu we could see the fireworks over downtown Shenzhen and over the Tsing Ma bridge in Hong Kong, and on satellite TV we watched the small crowds gathered in Statue Square, waving the new Hong Kong flag—the one with the purple flower, the *bauhinnia.* The joke is, I told her, that it's a hybrid flower, and it's sterile. Produces no offspring. But she didn't laugh. In the flickering light of the screen, her face was inert, unmoved; nothing I did made her smile.

I'm sorry, she said. I'm just tired.

You need to look for another job. A day job. This work isn't right for you.

I don't see what they're celebrating, she said, nodding at the screen. Hasn't it been a terrible year? What about the stock market crash?

They're celebrating the future, then. Things will get better.

The future, she said. What a luxury.

I turned off the TV, and we sat slumped on the couch in the dark.

I'm sorry. She touched my knee. I feel like I've poisoned you.

We have to forget all this, I said. Can't we just be *us,* just once?

She reached for my hand and squeezed it, hard. I want to, she said. Try to make me forget.

When it was over she folded herself against me, limp, like a body washed in by the tide.

I have an idea, I said, the next morning, bringing her a cup of tea in bed. I want you to hear me out. Will you listen?

She nodded, brushing hair out of her eyes.

I've been reading some articles about immigration, I said. We both know there's no way to move you forward on the list for Hong Kong. And I can't legally change my residence to the mainland—even if you wanted me to. But there's nothing to stop us from simultaneously emigrating to a third country.

But—

I raised my hand. There are two options for us, I said. Canada and Australia. Both are expensive. I would have to sell my parents' investments. And we would probably have to wait two or three years for you to get a visa. But that's it—three years at the most. You could start a Chinese kindergarten in Toronto or Vancouver or Sydney. It wouldn't be so hard—I could help you.

You would do that? Leave Hong Kong for good?

Not necessarily for good. Once you're naturalized in another country we can move back to Hong Kong if we want to. We'll keep my apartment and rent it out.

She drank her tea in one gulp and set the cup down. You've figured everything out, she said. Haven't you.

It's not so difficult. People do it all the time.

Of course, she said. People buy wives all the time.

Her eyes were bloodshot, and there was a streak of rouge smeared across her nose. And I felt I couldn't tolerate her stubbornness for a moment longer. It seemed perverse, even artificial, and I felt myself getting angry, a rim of hot sweat around my lips.

The rest of the world isn't Shenzhen, I said. You don't have to see it that way. *We* don't have to see it that way. Once you've left China everything will be different.

She gave a small cry, like a cat when you step on its paw, and reached over and slapped me across the face. Don't tell me about the rest of the world! she shouted. Don't tell me what you can do for me. Is that what love is? She moved to the other side of the bed and stood up, winding the sheet around her. No more, she said. I'm almost out of money. I have to move out of my room.

You didn't tell me that.

I'm getting rid of my mobile, she said. I'm leaving my job.

What will you do?

Don't ask me that question.

Lin, I said, don't I deserve an answer?

She turned to the window, covering her face with her hands,

the sheet sagging around her ankles. You should forget about me, she said hoarsely, her voice muffled in her palms. I warned you. You should never have expected anything from me.

I don't believe you, I said. I know what you want. You only have to be brave and want it *enough*.

She took a corner of the sheet and wrapped it again around her chest, and blew her nose with her fingers, the way farmers do. It isn't a question of bravery, she said. You still don't understand.

I blinked my eyes once, twice; the room seemed to bend around me, like a reflection in one of those funny mirrors at Ocean Park. Lin, I said, it doesn't matter who has the money and who doesn't. If I were in your position—

If I lived in Hong Kong, you would never have noticed me, she said, turning from the window. You wouldn't have looked at me twice. Isn't that true?

No, I said, but I felt a sagging weight in my chest, as if I had swallowed a stone. Of course it was true. I saw myself again in the dark back corner of the Club Nikko, handing her a packet of tissues, a business card—when would I have done that, in my normal life, with a stranger? *It isn't important,* I wanted to say. *How can it be so important?* But the words wouldn't form on my tongue. I saw my face as she must have seen it: my eyebrows tilted in concern, my mouth slowly forming the syllables, as if I were talking to a child. I hadn't meant to sound that way, I thought. But how else could she have heard it?

Pity isn't love, she said, her voice dropping to a whisper. It doesn't turn into love. Maybe I thought it could, but I was wrong. I'm sorry if I deceived you.

This can't be the end, I said weakly. I sat down on the edge of the bed, steadying myself with my hands; the floor seemed to fall away from me, curving into the trough of a wave. For a moment I thought I would be sick. *You are making a terrible mistake,* I wanted to shout. *You'll always regret this.* But I knew how she would respond. *I made that mistake already.*

I think you're lying to me, I shouted at her suddenly. I wasn't even aware of what I was saying; I only felt my shoulders clenched together, as if I were expecting the ceiling to fall. You're not really out of a job, are you? You're just sick of me and you want someone else. It's a convenient excuse, isn't it?

She turned and stared at me, and a shiver of recognition ran down her body: as if I had confirmed something she had always known. I'm going home, she said. Back to Anhui. Maybe I'll get a job. Probably not. I don't care if I have to eat rice out of a hole in the ground. At least I won't be one of those women who sits in a villa and waits for a man, like a wind-up toy. I may go crazy, but not that way.

We took a taxi together from Nanhai Lu into the city, and at a street corner, just blocks away from the border, she told the driver to stop and got out quickly, without saying a word. Hey! the driver shouted. Pay your fare!

It's all right, I said. I'm paying for both of us.

As I walked to the border terminal, the clouds were beginning to break up, and the sidewalks glowed in the glaring sun. Twenty minutes later, when the train pulled out of the station on the Hong Kong side, I rested my forehead against the cool glass of the window and closed my eyes. I knew exactly how I wanted to remember her: sitting on the plastic couch, her feet propped up, her hair still wet from the shower, laughing at some inane romantic comedy on the TV. I strained to fix the image in my mind, but already it was difficult to recall the details: what did she do with her hands? How did her voice sound when she spoke my name?

If I disappear, that's it, she had said. *China will swallow me up.*

Finally I gave up and opened my eyes.

When you take the train south from the border into Hong Kong, after you pass the small town of Sheung Shui, the countryside opens up into a lush valley, a lowland forest dotted with small farms that climb the sides of gently sloping hills. This is the valley of Fanling. In all my trips past this place, I had never seen what I was passing: a hundred shades of green so rich and deep that it hurt my eyes to look at them. In the colonial days, I read once, the English governors and magistrates had huge estates in Fanling, and they played a game where they released a fox and then chased after it with horses and a pack of dogs. All the animals had to be imported from England—even the fox! But it was worth it to them, because it was the same game that they played at home in England, and they wanted to forget for a morning that they were here, instead of there. I wondered what it would feel like to ride a horse through that incredible landscape, so green that it hurt your eyes to see it, and whether one of those Englishmen might have slowed his horse for a moment, and breathed the air, and felt in that instant that he belonged *here,* on the other side of the world from where he was born. I raised my head from the window, and the faces of the other passengers dissolved, as if I were looking at them from underwater; and I whispered to myself, *Peace, peace, peace.*

Marston Lodge, Long Marston, County of York

All the land around us belongs to Major York.
Also the house we live in, the barn behind,
the swineherd's hut beyond that. Also his
the apple trees in the orchard and every apple,
even the windfalls rotting softly in the deep grass.
His, each pheasant hen in the brush and all her chicks,
every trembling rabbit in the hedge, even the shallow
pond filling too slowly against encroaching cattails
and the black-billed coots who paddle the still surface.
Blasted oak, stark sentry at the lane's end, its beefsteak
mushroom livid as a scar; the nettles rank along
the roadside, knee-deep at the garden's edge,
the circle of wild mushrooms near the midden, all his.
His, the surrounding flat fields of oats to the south,
long columns of currant bushes rising over the swell
of the land to the east, regular as militia. His, stacked
bales of hay outside the empty barn. As far as
the next village, his lands and all thereon.

Ours, sunlight that stripes the floor of the byre
mornings when the kettle is put to boil for tea,
the dreams of field mice who winter under the stairs.
Ours, wind off the moors snapping sheets, rippling
in summer the slender stalks of early oats
to silver green, whistling over the garden wall
driving before it slant needles of rain. Ours,
the call of rooks in the field early mornings
as we tend our vegetables, weeding and hoeing,
earthing the celery and asparagus.

My Wife

My wife's younger brother took heroin and died
in the bed he slept in as a boy across
the hall from the one she slept in as a girl.

He sold the pot he grew in their basement and
she'd leave work to take him to rehab
but their father was the unhappiest child
in their house and she had to save herself.

No one changes what happens to them.
History is the story of one unhappy family
and a family is a group of strangers who live together.

Two months after he died, we hold hands
across a black sea, trying not to despise
the drunk at the next table, who doesn't
even try not to listen. It's best not to think
about the pain. To shut your eyes and float.

Before I met my wife I'd put on anything clean.
My life was a heavy shadow, dragging behind.
I was resigned to anonymity. I wanted to sleep.
My wife gave my pain a bride.

Our kids were jumping on our bed, windmilling,
when she answered the phone and sighed
and shut her eyes and sat down, the words
reaching all the way down into her soul.

He was a sweet young man who came over
and hugged us at our wedding, and looked,
when we took him on his thirtieth birthday
to a restaurant filled with beautiful women,
as if he wanted to live forever.

When we visited his grave, the kids and I
wandered around in a city of the dead
and I could see her down the long avenues,
pulling weeds and staring at the ground.

At night she walks in the dark downstairs.
I know what she wants, to go to him the way
she goes to our boys when they're frightened,
to undo all the wrong so he can sleep.

Fire in a Jar

Some plucked from flight by sweep of net
or grasp of hand, immediately darken
and flicker out. A drift of stars becomes
mere green beetles scraping the glass bottom
of a jar. Other kinds go on flashing, ardent
no matter how captive they are, lighting
up even the smallest heaven. And still
others make a haze of their own longing,
dispersing themselves into a diffuse haze,
becoming a drop of sexual sunlight falling
upon the transparent world. Glass eye,
glass heart, glass jar, in which we try and keep
our flickering selves, all the light in us is sexual,
a luminous persistence—a heaven or a hell.

REGINALD SHEPHERD

Somewhere Outside of Eden

for Robert Philen

I saw all these things the moment
contained (what the light
proposed), a camellia bush
in thick red bloom all January, some
flowers browning on the dormant
lawn (still green): they smelled like something
afternoon; wax baskets of evergreen
mistletoe hung from bare limbs
of a southern red oak, verdant
parasite on the sleeping life, a full complement
of complementary colors.

The three o'clock half-moon
dangled above still-lifes of tree grass house
like a quarter shoved in a slot, we passed
an empty lot where two azalea
bushes and a spreading live oak
marked the place a homestead
had been; a steep voice tumbled down
a slope of lawn (we'd walked
right into March), only a mockingbird
perched in the heights of a naked tree
on the periphery of day.

When you said, *Let's go home,*
I answered, *Where is that.*

Commuters

Something in this long commute
is chilling. The street between
Karlin and Nessen City's broken,
carnage is literal and fresh:
raccoon, a deer new since yesterday,
crow, loose feathers desultory
in the jet stream of a car.
This afternoon a mallard looks
more human in death
than he ever did bobbing
on a pond: face-down, feet
splayed, last-second intelligence
in the curve of his neck.
The sun bears down on this,
or the rain, or whatever,
tallied by the oil trucks, retreads,
the dry accumulation of salt
and dirt along the quarter panels,
crusting the body from hood
to rear, and all about this
business has the raw stink of oil,
all of it: the lawyer's tie,
the paper the lease is written on,
the candy bars for lunch,
the squat offices, the flat,
blank windows. The stench
of oil, yes, all of it has that,
the music on tape, the oil
paints, the latex, the truckload
of kiln-dried pine, pulled with

buzzing saws from Arctic Ontario,
Rowan's grocery with the Teamsters
delivery tractor rumbling at
the loading bay, yes, even the music ·
reeks with oil, the dead trumpeter,
his horn shoots a gusher.

CATHY SONG

The Souls We Carry Hunger for Our Light

The souls we carry hunger for our light.
They who feel unfortunate, close in
on the fields, convene around happiness.
They hear the sound of it like laughter,
on roads, through rain-blurred trees,
the smell of it boiled through bones
and cartilage, the taste of earth
deep and darkly rooted.

Drawn to those sleeping skin to skin,
they shiver, wanting fur, wanting in,
the closeness of animals
sharing heat, sharing fire.
They want to be let back in.

The muscular ache of the man splitting wood,
the muscular ache of the woman
tidying the beds of messy children,
bring desire for tenderness so intense
they would gladly return home
to houses that indifferently bred them.

The souls we carry hunger for our light,
the music of that open door calling them
as they thrash through realms of enslavement
thick as honey.
It's the first bite of sweetness they crave,
and the last.
Gathered around the kitchen table
they thrill to the clamoring.
They remember the woman sighing
open her blouse and the man cutting into pieces
small mouthfuls of his own sweet cake.

Dead, You Can Keep Going

Arturo stomps the heel of his boot and tells me:
Every *pinche* minute I mess up a red ant. That's no good,

I tell him, me the young man in the next row,
The shadow of my hoe cutting weeds in Boswell's beet field.

Arturo says: every super *pinche* half-hour I see this squirrel spin
And drop—you know, the chemicals you and me are breathing.

That's not nice, I tell him and hold my breath for a long second.
I then feel something touch my sleeve—

Sunlight where there was dark and the icy thread of stars.
We started before dawn, as the tainted valley wind nudged us along

And I had no thoughts other than counting my steps.
Now morning has peeled its eye open. Blackbirds follow

Our shoe prints, scolding us with hard, clapper-like tongues.
My anger is fired up by weeds and blackbirds in their judges' robes,

And the shouting at my house
Where we five kids grow like weeds ourselves,

Cut down by the anger of Mother's hot iron,
A stepfather's glare through a shot glass licked of bourbon.

I think of home, far to the east
And remember the sea that I once heard when I put a can to my ear

And heard a storm I liked. Then a blackbird shouts
And Arturo, steps ahead, says: every morning I say my *pinche* prayers

And I'm still in hell. He spits words I can't make out, or care about.
I stop when the long tooth of my hoe divides

One of those thin-waisted red ants. I stop, hunch down,
And study its jaws still gripping its load.

Poor guy, I think. I raise his back legs onto my finger
And notice even dead you can keep going,

For this halved red ant is still kicking.
Righted, his legs circle the whorls of my fingerprints

And then stagger down the length of this digit,
Falling where the weeds fall back into the wind-tipped row.

Bio

What it was like to sit with Mr. Fox
on the Blvd. Raspail and negotiate
my post at Morlais, then Toulouse, then come back
in a riveted trunk with Henry Millers sewn
into my lining, Frank Sinatra to greet me
in the mile square city, Dutch ships everywhere
my father and mother in from Pittsburgh to give me
my French lesson, my fiancée pulling me down,
the mayor of New York god knows who, the president
asinine again, the dove I loved
in an army boot size eleven and a half and
dove or not, dove feathers or not, blood staining
the white chest, a cascade of snow come pouring
from the spruce's upper limbs, cascade, waterfall,
sheet, blanket, my mountain, your roof, your dovecote,
eating fish on the *Times*, 103rd Street,
Zoey in a corset, even then she
was a throwback—I have unlaced a corset,
and at a vanity I have sat on a stained
bench and broken my knees against art dreco
peeling wood, and there among the powders
and creams and rouges I have read Montaigne,
Locke, and Hobbes, and since it was there, I read
the rituals of the Eastern Star and studied
my face in the unsilvered mirror, what about you?

Alchemy

Stone turns to buttermilk, pipe-
cleaners to dreams, necromancers
and pythons to aristocrats
and ballerinas. Here Platinum

shrinks lung cancer. Taxol,
from tree bark, withers
an ovarian metastasis into nothingness
and Prednisone, cures lymphoma.

What is this, then, if not alchemy,
potions and witch's brews,
toxins turned to gold, barbed wire
into silvery South Sea pearls.

ROBERT SULLIVAN

Tane Retrieves the Baskets of Knowledge

I shimmied my way up the thick vine like a cord
plugged into heaven—electricity crackled down the line
between my hands, reflexes tightening the fingers—I took it
as a message from the gods, onwards! So up I went

clapping hands ankles knees to the breeze
as the cord arced left and right in the sky—
I climbed this thought all the way until I reached
Io The Parentless One, the supreme deity.

Without moving his lips he asked me how I got there.
"Oh great lord, it was a thought
that carried me here, and a thought that will
return me to my family." Young man,

my creatures helped you here: the wind god
Tawhirimatea launched your body and your thought;
I let you visualize the vine; now you are here
so that you may carry these baskets of thoughts

back to your family so they may call themselves gods,
and launch houses of knowledge. Take all three
and share them. If I could I'd pour them in your ears
but there's too many: they could spill over the minds

of evil men so take great care of them: secrets
to split the atom; secrets to rule a country with expensive housing,
health care, and forcing people to fight; secret pollutants;
secrets to clone people; secret hate. Take great care

on your return, young man. "But lord, where is the vine I dreamt of?"
"E Tane, you see that arch in the clouds? Go through that door,
it leads to the eleven lower heavens to your home
on the ground."

"Your vine disappeared when you saw the baskets.
They contain all the thinking you will ever need.
Don't get me wrong—I liked your thought—maybe
your descendants will find one, too, and also climb it."

Ocean Birth

With the leaping spirits we threw
        our voices past Three Kings to sea—
                eyes wide open with ancestors.

We flew air and water, lifted
        by rainbows, whales, dolphins thrashing
                sharks into birthways of the sea's

labor: Rapanui born graven
        faced above the waves—umbilical
                stone; Tahiti born from waka:

temple center of the world;
        Hawai'i cauled from liquid
                fire: the goddess Pele churning

land from sea: born as mountains;
        Aotearoa on a grandmother's
                bone—Maui's blood to birth leviathan;

Samoa, Tonga, born before
        the names of the sea of islands,
                before Lapita clay turned to gourd,

before we slept with Pacific
        tongues. Chant these births Oceania
                with your infinite waves, outrigged

waka, bird feasts, and sea feasts,
        Peruvian gold potatoes.
                Sing your births Oceania.

Hold your children to the sky
        and sing them to the skyfather
                in the languages of your people.

Sing your songs Oceania.
        Pacific Islanders sing! till
                your throats are stones heaped as temples

on the shores for our ancestors'
        pleasure. PI's sing! to remind
                wave sand tree cliff cave of the songs

we left for the Moana Nui
        a Kiwa. We left our voices
                here in every singing bird—

trunks like drums—stones like babies—
        forests fed by our placentas.
                Every wave carries us here—

every song to remind us—
        we are skin of the ocean.

ARTHUR SZE

Chrysalis

Corpses push up through thawing permafrost,

as I scrape salmon skin off a pan at the sink;
on the porch, motes in slanting yellow light

undulate in air. Is Venus at dusk as luminous
as Venus at dawn? Yesterday I was about to

seal a borax capsule angled up from the bottom

of a decaying exterior jamb when I glimpsed
jagged ice floating in a bay. Naval sonar

slices through whales, even as a portion
of male dorsal fin is served to the captain

of an umiak. Stopped in traffic, he swings from

a chairlift, gazes down at scarlet paintbrush.
Moistening an envelope before sealing it,

I recall the slight noise you made when I
grazed your shoulder. When a frost wiped out

the chalk-blue flowering plant by the door,

I watered until it revived from the roots.
The song of a knife sharpener in an alley

passes through the mind of a microbiologist
before he undergoes anesthesia for surgery.

The first night of autumn has singed

bell peppers by the fence, while budding
chamisa stalks in the courtyard bend to ground.

Observing people conversing at another table,
he surmises this moment is the convergence

and divergence of lines passing through a point.

The wisteria along the porch has never bloomed;
a praying mantis on the wood floor sips water

from a dog bowl. Laughter from upstairs echoes
downstairs as teenage girls compare bra sizes.

A literary critic frets over the composition

of a search committee, utters contemptuous
remarks regarding potential applicants.

A welder, who turns away for a few seconds
to gaze at the Sangre de Cristos, detects a line

of trucks backed up on an international overpass

where exhaust spews onto houses below.
The day may be called One Toothroad or Six Thunderpain,

but a Mayan naming of a day will not transform it,
nor will the mathematics of time halt.

An imprint of ginkgo leaf—fan-shaped, slightly

thickened, slightly wavy on broad edge, two-
lobed, with forking parallel veins but no

mid-vein—in a slab of coal is momentary beauty,
while ginkgoes along a street dropping gold

leaves are mindless beauty of the quotidian.

Once thought to be extinct, the ginkgo was
discovered in Himalayan monasteries and

propagated back into the world. Although I
cannot save a grasshopper singed by frost

trying to warm itself in sunlight on a walkway,

I ponder shadows of budding pink and orange
bougainvilleas on a wall. As masons level sand,

lay bricks in horizontal then vertical pairs,
we construct a ground to render a space

our own. As light from a partial lunar eclipse

diffuses down skylight walls, we rock and
sluice, rock and sluice, fingertips fanned

to fanned fingertips, debouch into plentitude.
Venus vanishes in a brightening sky: how long

does a diamond ring of a solar eclipse persist?

You did not have to fly to Zimbabwe in June 2001
to experience it. The day recalls Thirteen Death

and One Deer when an end slips into a beginning.
I recall mating butterflies with red dots on wings,

the bow of a long liner thudding on waves,

crescendo of water beginning to boil in a kettle,
cries of humpback whales. In silence dancers

concentrate on movements on stage; lilacs bud
by a gate. As bits of consciousness constellate,

I rouse to a three a.m. December rain on the skylight.

A woman sweeps glass shards in a driveway,
oblivious to elm branches reflected on windshields

of passing cars. Juniper crackles in the fireplace;
whale flukes break the water as it dives.

The path of totality is not marked by

a shadow hurtling across the earth's surface
at three thousand kilometers per hour,

but by our eyelashes attuned to each other.
At the mouth of an arroyo, a lamb skull

and rib cage bleach in the sand; tufts of fleece

caught on barbed wire have vanished.
The Shang carved characters in the skulls

of their enemies, but what transpired here?
You do not need to steep turtle shells

in blood to prognosticate clouds. Someone

dumps a refrigerator upstream in the riverbed
while you admire the yellow blossoms of

a golden rain tree. A woman weeds, sniffs
fragrance from a line of onions in her garden;

you scramble an egg, sip oolong tea.

The continuous bifurcates into the segmented
even as the broken extends into the continuous.

Someone swipes a newspaper while we snooze.
A tiger swallowtail lands on a patio columbine;

a single agaric breaks soil by a hollyhock.

Pushing aside branches of Russian olives
to approach the Pojoaque River, we stumble onto

a splatter of flicker feathers in the dirt.
Here chance and fate enmesh each other.

Here I hold a black bowl rinsed with tea,

savor the warmth at my fingertips,
aroma of emptiness. We rock back and forth,

back and forth on water. Fins of spinner
dolphins break the waves; a whale spouts

to the north-northwest. What is not impelled?

Yellow hibiscus, zodiac, hairbrush;
barbed wire, smog, snowflake—when I still

my eyes, the moments dilate. Rain has darkened
gravel in the courtyard; shriveled apples

on branches are weightless against dawn.

Refugees in Our Own Land

The night is busy with the growth of stars. Above us peaceful. Shiyáázh, *my son,* fusses in his cradleboard. The protective rainbow shaped by his father arches over his face to protect him. In the dark sand below Monster Slayer's archenemy rises again to pull us off this rock where we've taken refuge since winter's approach.

The wind stops. Clouds drift across the moon. We pull water silently from below near the soldier's feet. Silence is our cover. I pull my son close and place my hand on my baby's cheek to quiet him. Shhh, shee'awéé', shiyázhí, shhh. *Hush, baby, my beloved, hush.* With my finger I circle the pulse just above his ear. He makes tiny lapping sounds with his mouth and turns toward my breast for the comfort of my milk. But my breast is a sieve from which the enemy drinks. I am dry.

These hands mixed bread dough for the evening meal, planted corn, and gathered pollen from the tender shoots of corn. This hand held my husband's kisses and caressed my son's baby soft bones as he grew inside me. We sailed the river that led us to the ocean of all beginnings. The night cries like an owl. My beloved's eyes are full of stars. A drowning breath in his throat. Take this map of rainbows and fly, fly, baby.

Transatlantic

Lebanon, Nebraska

She stares through the window to the garden gate, guarded by
  Thunderbirds, one on each side, the road
leading out to the highway. *I'm waiting until I don't love you,* she
  answers. Puts her cup on its hook. Impossible to dry anything.
  Dishes, clothes. Your cheek
where the cat licks it clean. So much life other than our own
  loves the heat, the close nights crackling with starlight, you'd
  think we would grow fond of it.
You'd think that the locusts screaming from the trees, the alien
  sea everywhere, fecund and vicious, would make us grow fond
  of each other,
time running out like air from a tiny hole on a starship adrift in
  the darkness. So sad to grow old without family.
To face your own extinction without hope, or any accounting or
  appeal. So sad to love and not be loved even a little in return.

Beirut, Beirut

The kids at the New York Disco talk the talk but barely
remember the last time foreign flags flew here, though
everyone claims to know someone whose brother died a
martyr.

Everyone knows the difference between Coke and Pepsi, Fox and
CNN, the latest U.S. presidents and the ones that they
replaced.

One day we will rule the stars, booms the bouncer, a retired
colonel.

Just ask Little Mehmet, the adulterer, who spits like a camel
during Ramadan and eats sweet cakes in secret in the
afternoon.

Just ask "Jake," who manages the city's largest McDonald's
restaurant, the poor dressed up and the rich studiously
nonchalant, to explain the difference.

PAMELA   USCHUK

Remembering the Tet Offensive As
Troops Ship Out for a U.S. Attack on Iraq

for Roger C. Frank

A fighter jet etches ink white as sperm
on the stark sky while January troops deploy
from Camp LeJeune, just like my first husband
did in 1968 on his way to Viet Nam
to wipe the Commie Gooks off the map.
Before he could spell Khe Sahn, think
massacre, he was machine-gunned
then bayoneted, left to die two days
in a jungle valley of shimmering green bamboo
near the clear stream he couldn't reach
before the chop chop of the Medevac arrived.
One of three survivors of a whole company
of young marines slaughtered, he wanted to toss
The Purple Heart in the trash.
I remember during the long Michigan winter,
his night sweats, the way
he'd shout the apartment walls awake, shake
to the screams of his buddies as they choked
on their own blood, clotted by indifferent flies,
some disemboweled, legs
or arms, faces blasted like frosted poppies.
He'd point to the mean hieroglyphs of red scars,
a pinched cummerbund of bullet
and stab wounds cinching his waist,
then ask me, new bride, too young
to be a Sphinx, the riddle I couldn't reason out.
What was this for? What for?
as he headed to the kitchen for anesthetic beer,
the amber mattress of whiskey straight.
In three years he joined his company underground.
He was handsome, gung-ho like these teen soldiers

interviewed on CNN, cocky
as oiled M-16s, proclaiming
their belief as each generation before them
that they will fight the war to end all wars.
Behind them, wives and girlfriends wave
small American flags that break
in the brittle wind.

Up the Steps of the Capitol

In line with many strangers,
we were roughed-up bodies
ready for more. We clasped hands.
A song made us iron. The line of us
could walk and sing. The line of us went on
and on—up the steps of the capitol and out
into towns with quarter-inch phone books.
Some in line knew the gods
and some their vices and others
how much was required of us
or just how rough it was
about to get. And the line of us
shrugged when we heard. We
were iron. From the purest
ore. This was after warnings
but before forbidding. Before
the dead came in waves, heavier
each time in our arms. Before
we had no hand free to close their eyes.
Still, for a while the rain seemed
nothing. We lashed ourselves
to ourselves. We were a line. Un-
crossable. The line of us could walk
and weep and believe we were of use.

G. C. WALDREP

The Little Man in the Fire Hates Me

There is not so much water here as pollen.

A lesson in obedience, in Victorian industry:
I am busy, busy   therefore the child will live.
Sheets blossoming like crucified roses.
I beg the silk of a single petal. Am denied.
You will not need this currency for your particular journey.

I return to the stove.
The boiling pot is neither abstract nor demure.
It is hissing its elementary decalogue.

True: I am embarrassed by the fact of the book.
False: I regret it.

Sometimes I linger, sometimes not.
No cries come from the next room.
But I am still trying to believe. The incarnation, the thrust.
And what becomes of that other.
Exhausted. Viviparous.
Salt rising like a buzz from the invection.
A lowering.

Everyone wants to fuse a tragic story to his own, after the fact.

bergamot, turk's cap, spiderwort, yarrow, foamflower
(fire-pink dying—
(pink orchids, where you waited—

There is a third cell in the eye that witnesses to the light.
When voice fails, the body substitutes.

Taking Out Trash

There's more to it than spilling our red garbage can
into the city's big blue bin. I have to slip
from bed without waking my wife. (I pretend

I'm a silk handkerchief, the bed's a pocket;
then I pick myself.) I sneak past my children's
bedrooms, where they lie submerged in sleep.

Easing shut the kitchen door, I stuff yesterday's
news in the recycling bag. I dump
the pork chow mein my wife brought home

from lunch, and forgot to refrigerate.
After sponging the placemats (apricot-cake crumbs,
dry scraps of beef our toddler missed),

I wash a dish of congealed oatmeal down
the sink, and toss the junk mail
I left out to "think about." (Should I compare

insurance rates? Would anyone I know enjoy
a *Gone with the Wind* porcelain egg?)
I scratch the cat's ears, replenish her liver-

and-shrimp, sift the offerings from her cat box,
and drop them in the Hefty-bag-lined
garbage can. When our gate squeaks,

I think (as usual), "I've got to oil that,"
as I consign the Hefty bag to the blue bin.
Back in the house, I close the door quietly,

turn on the furnace, and by its proxy,
nudge my family awake with a warm hand—
I, who used to wear my guitar like a chasuble,

invoking God through a Shure microphone.
I: a former stand-in for Zeppelin and The Stones,
who thought he was a most important man.

Sentence

Look:

paper screen

blank;

the color white,

a zero,

hollow light bulb,

the O   not yet typed.

This means

no imagination
without
its *imagery*.

Letters   can appear

as bones

(Do not forget the image)

if you   write with   calcium.

Because a subject

can be half a skeleton,

the verb, the other half

and the skull,

a period.

Cautionary Tale

Twenty-one once descript ranch-style houses built twenty years ago on a stretch of road that once led to a small-time chicken farm, fresh eggs. Each house dropped on two bare acres. Twenty-one tabula rasas that go *wish wish wish wish* if racing by with a car window down. No one has ever slammed on their brakes right in the middle of the wishing, backed up, pulled over, turned off the engine, gotten out. There's the tiniest sign posted on the split rail fence in front of the 11th house. It claims that the house is located exactly halfway between the city of Reeling and the town of Boon. Not only that. The house lies right on the town/city line—half on one side, half on the other. The Boon side is painted black; the Reeling, white. Black and white, at times the world offers too much. Who lives in that house? An unknown number of squatters. Here's what's on their round table: whether to lock or leave unlocked the front door at night. And lingering inside, this latest response: *"What's happened to us that this is our greatest worry? The house isn't even ours."*

XU XI

Famine

I escape. I board Northwest 18 to New York, via Tokyo. The engine starts, there is no going back. Yesterday, I taught the last English class and left my job of thirty-two years. Five weeks earlier, A-Ma died of heartbreak, within days of my father's sudden death. He was ninety-five, she ninety. Unlike A-Ba, who saw the world by crewing on tankers, neither my mother nor I ever left Hong Kong.

Their deaths rid me of responsibility at last, and I could forfeit my pension and that dreary existence. I am fifty-one and an only child, unmarried.

I never expected my parents to take so long to die.

This meal is *luxurious,* better than anything I imagined.

My colleagues who fly every summer complain of the indignities of travel. Cardboard food, cramped seats, long lines, and these days, too much security nonsense, they say. They fly Cathay, our "national" carrier. This makes me laugh. We have never been a nation; "national" isn't our adjective. *Semantics,* they say, dismissive, just as they dismiss what I say of debt, that it is not an inevitable state, or that children exist to be taught, not spoilt. My colleagues live in overpriced, new, mortgaged flats and indulge 1 to 2.5 children. Most of my students are uneducable.

Back, though, to this in-flight meal. Smoked salmon and cold shrimp, endive salad, strawberries and melon to clean the palate. Then, steak with mushrooms, potatoes *au gratin,* a choice between a shiraz or cabernet sauvignon. Three cheeses, white chocolate mousse, coffee and port or a liqueur or brandy. Foods from the pages of a novel, perhaps.

My parents ate sparingly, long after we were no longer impoverished, and disdained "unhealthy" Western diets. A-Ba often said that the only thing he really discovered from travel was that the world was hungry, and that there would never be enough food for everyone. It was why, he said, he did not miss the travel when he retired.

I have no complaints of my travels so far.

My complaining colleagues do not fly business. This seat is an *island* of a bed, surrounded by air. I did not mean to fly in dignity, but having never traveled in summer, or at all, I didn't plan months ahead, long before flights filled up. I simply rang the airlines and booked Northwest, the first one that had a seat, only in business class.

Friends and former students, who do fly business when their companies foot the bill, were horrified. *You* paid *full fare? No one does!* I have money, I replied, why shouldn't I? *But you've given up your "rice bowl." Think of the future.*

I hate rice, always have, even though I never left a single grain, because under my father's watchful glare, A-Ma inspected my bowl. Every meal, even after her eyes dimmed.

The Plaza Suite is nine hundred square feet, over three times the size of home. I had wanted the Vanderbilt or Ambassador and would have settled for the Louis XV, but they were all booked, by those more important than I, no doubt. Anyway, this will have to do. "Nothing unimportant" happens here at the Plaza is what their website literature claims.

The porter arrives, and wheels my bags in on a trolley.

My father bought our tiny flat in a village in Shatin with his disability settlement. When he was fifty and I one, a falling crane crushed his left leg and groin, thus ending his sailing and procreating career. Shatin isn't very rural anymore, but our home has denied progress its due. We didn't get a phone till I was in my thirties.

I tip the porter five dollars and begin unpacking the leather luggage set. There is too much space for my things.

Right about now, you're probably wondering, along with my colleagues, former students, and friends, *What on earth does she think she's doing?* It was what my parents shouted when I was twelve and went on my first hunger strike.

My parents were illiterate, both refugees from China's rural poverty. A-Ma fried tofu at Shatin market. Once A-Ba recovered from his accident, he worked there also as a cleaner, cursing his fate. They expected me to support them as soon as possible, which should have been after six years of primary school, the only compulsory education required by law in the sixties.

As you see, I clearly had no choice but to strike, since my exam results proved I was smart enough for secondary school. My father beat me, threatened to starve me. *How dare I,* when others were genuinely hungry, unlike me, the only child of a tofu seller who always ate. *Did I want him and A-Ma to die of hunger just to send me to school? How dare I risk their longevity and old age?*

But I was unpacking a Spanish leather suitcase when the past, that country bumpkin's territory, so rudely interrupted.

Veronica, whom I met years ago at university while taking a literature course, foisted this luggage on me. She runs her family's garment enterprise, and is married to a banker. Between them and their three children, they own four flats, three cars, and at least a dozen sets of luggage. Veronica invites me out to dinner (she always pays) whenever she wants to complain about her family. Lately, we've dined often.

"Kids," she groaned over our rice porridge, two days before my trip. "My daughter won't use her brand-new Loewe set because, she says, that's *passé.* All her friends at Stanford sling these canvas bags with one fat strap. Canvas, imagine. Not even leather."

"Ergonomics," I told her, annoyed at this bland and inexpensive meal. "It's all about weight and balance." And cost, I knew, because the young overspend to conform, just as Veronica eats rice porridge because she's overweight and no longer complains that I'm thin.

She continued. "You're welcome to take the set if you like."

"Don't worry yourself. I can use an old school bag."

"But that's barely a cabin bag! Surely not enough to travel with."

In the end, I let her nag me into taking this set which is more bag than clothing.

Veronica sounded worried when I left her that evening. "Are you *sure* you'll be okay?"

And would she worry, I wonder, if she could see me now, here, in this suite, this enormous space where one night's bill would have taken my parents years, no, *decades,* to earn and even for me, four years' pay, at least when I first started teaching in my rural enclave (though you're thinking, of course, quite correctly, *Well, what about inflation,* the thing economists cite to dismiss these longings of an English teacher who has spent her life instructing those who care not a whit for our "official language," the one they never speak, at least not if they can choose, especially not now when there is, increasingly, a choice).

My unpacking is done; the past need not intrude. I draw a bath, as one does in English Literature, to wash away the heat and grime of both cities in summer. *Why New York?* Veronica asked, at the end of our last evening together. Because, I told her, it will be like nothing I've ever known. For the first time since we've known each other, Veronica actually seemed to envy *me*, although perhaps it was my imagination.

The phone rings, and it's "Guest Relations" wishing to welcome me and offer hospitality. The hotel must wonder, since I grace no social register. I ask for a table at Lutèce tonight. Afterwards, I tip the concierge ten dollars for successfully making the reservation. As you can see, I am no longer an ignorant bumpkin, even though I never left the schools in the New Territories, our urban countryside, now that no one farms anymore. Besides, Hong Kong magazines detail lives of the rich and richer so I've read of the famous restaurant and know about the greasy palms of New Yorkers.

I order tea and scones from Room Service. It will hold me till dinner at eight.

The first time I ever tasted tea and scones was at the home of my private student. To supplement income when I enrolled in Teacher Training, I tutored Form V students who needed to pass the School Certificate English exam. This was the compromise I agreed to with my parents before they would allow me to qualify as a teacher. Oh yes, there was a second hunger strike two years prior, before they would let me continue into Form IV. That time, I promised to keep working in the markets after school with A-Ma, which I did.

Actually, my learning English at all was a stroke of luck, since I was *hardly* at a "name school" of the elite. An American priest taught at my secondary school, so I heard a native speaker. He wasn't a very good teacher, but he paid attention to me because I was the only student who liked the subject. A little attention goes a long way.

Tea and scones! I am *supposed* to be eating, not dwelling on the ancient past. The opulence of the tray Room Service brings far surpasses what that pretentious woman served, mother of the hopeless boy, my first private student of many, who only passed his English exam because he cheated (he paid a friend to sit the exam for him), not that I'd ever tell since he's now a wealthy international businessman of some repute who can hire staff to communicate in English with the rest of the world, since he still cannot, at least not with any credibility. That scone ("from Cherikoff," she bragged) was cold and dry, hard as a rock.

Hot scones, oozing with butter. To ooze. I like the lasciviousness of that word, with its excess of vowels, the way an excess of wealth allows people to waste kindness on me, as my former student still does, every lunar new year, by sending me a *laisee* packet with a generous check which I deposit in my parents' bank account, the way I surrender all my earnings, as any filial and responsible unmarried child should, or so they said.

I eat two scones oozing with butter and savor tea enriched by cream and sugar, here at this "greatest hotel in the world," to vanquish, once and for all, my parents' fear of death and opulence.

Eight does not come soon enough. In the taxi on the way to Lutèce, I ponder the question of pork.

When we were poor but not impoverished, A-Ma once dared to make pork for dinner. It was meant to be a treat, to give me a taste of meat, because I complained that tofu was bland. A-Ba became a vegetarian after his accident and prohibited meat at home; eunuchs are angry people. She dared because he was not eating with us that night, a rare event in our family (I think some sailors he used to know invited him out).

I shat a tapeworm the next morning—almost ten inches long— and she never cooked pork again.

I have since tasted properly cooked pork, naturally, since it's unavoidable in Chinese cuisine. In my twenties, I dined out with friends, despite my parents' objections. But friends marry and scatter; the truth is that there is no one but family in the end, so over time, I submitted to their way of being and seldom took meals away from home, meals my mother cooked virtually till the day she died.

I am distracted. The real question, of course, is whether or not I should order pork tonight.

I did not expect this trip to be fraught with pork!

At Lutèce, I have the distinct impression that the two couples at the next table are talking about me. Perhaps they pity me. People often pitied me my life. *Starved of affection,* they whispered, although why they felt the need to whisper what everyone could hear I failed to understand. All I desired was greater gastronomic variety, but my parents couldn't bear the idea of my eating without them. I ate our plain diet and endured their perpetual skimping because they did eventually learn to leave me alone. That much filial propriety was reasonable payment. I just didn't expect them to *stop* complaining, to fear for what little fortune they had, because somewhere someone was less fortunate than they. That fear made them cling hard to life, forcing me to suffer their fortitude, their good health, and their longevity.

I should walk over to those overdressed people and tell them how things are, about famine, I mean, the way I tried to tell my students, the way my parents dinned it into me as long as they were alive.

Famine has no menu! The waiter waits as I take too long to study the menu. He does not seem patient, making him an oxymoron in his profession. My students would no more learn the oxymoron than they would learn about famine. *Daughter, did you lecture your charges today about famine?* A-Ba would ask every night before dinner. *Yes,* I learned to lie, giving him the answer he needed. This waiter could take a lesson in patience from me.

Finally, I look up at this man who twitches, and do not order pork. *Very good,* he says, as if I should be graded for my literacy in menus. He returns shortly with a bottle of the most expensive red available, and now I *know* the people at the next table are staring. The minute he leaves, the taller of the two men from that table comes over.

"Excuse me, but I believe we met in March? At the U.S. Consulate cocktail in Hong Kong? You're Kwai-sin Ho, aren't you?" He extends his hand. "Peter Martin."

Insulted, it's my turn to stare at this total stranger. I look *nothing* like that simpering socialite who designs wildly fashionable hats that are all the rage in Asia. Hats! We don't have the weather for hats, especially not those things, which are good for neither warmth nor shelter from the sun.

Besides, what use are hats for the hungry?

I do not accept his hand. "I'm her twin sister," I lie. "Kwai-sin and I are estranged."

He looks like he's about to protest, but retreats. After that, they don't stare, although I am sure they discuss me now that I've contributed new gossip for those who are nurtured by the crumbs of the rich and famous. But at least I can eat in peace.

It's my outfit, probably. Kwai-sin Ho is famous for her *cheongsams,* which is all she ever wears, the way I do. It was my idea. When we were girls together in school, I said the only thing I'd ever wear when I grew up was the *cheongsam,* the shapely dress with side slits and a neck-strangling collar. She grimaced and said they weren't fashionable, that only spinster schoolteachers and prostitutes wore them, which, back in the sixties, wasn't exactly true, but Kwai-sin was never too bright or imaginative.

That was long ago, before she became Kwai-sin in the *cheongsam* once these turned fashionable again, long before her father died and her mother became the mistress of a prominent businessman who whisked them into the stratosphere high above mine. For a little while, she remained my friend, but then we grew up, she married one of the shipping Hos, and became the socialite who refused, albeit politely, to recognize me the one time we bumped into each other at some function in Hong Kong.

So now, vengeance is mine. I will not entertain the people who fawn over her and possess no powers of recognition.

Food is getting sidelined by memory. This is unacceptable. I cannot allow all these intrusions. I must get back to the food, which is, after all, the point of famine.

This is due to a lack of diligence, as A-Ma would say, this lazy meandering from what's important, this succumbing to sloth. My mother was terrified of sloth, almost as much as she was terrified of my father.

She used to tell me an old legend about sloth.

There once was a man so lazy he wouldn't even lift food to his mouth. When he was young, his mother fed him, but as his mother aged, she couldn't. So he marries a woman who will feed him as his mother did. For a time, life is bliss.

Then one day, his wife must return to her village to visit her dying mother. "How will I eat?" he exclaims in fright. The wife conjures this plan. She bakes a gigantic cookie and hangs it on a string around his neck. All the lazy man must do is bend forward and eat. "Wonderful!" he says, and off she goes, promising to return.

On the first day, the man nibbles the edge of the cookie. Each day, he nibbles further. By the fourth day, he's eaten so far down there's no more cookie unless he turns it, which his wife expected he would since he could do this with his mouth.

However, the man's so lazy he lies down instead and waits for his wife's return. As the days pass, his stomach growls and begins to eat itself. Yet the man still won't turn the cookie. By the time his wife comes home, the lazy man has starved to death.

Memory causes such unaccountable digressions! There I was in Lutèce, noticing that people pitied me. Pity made my father livid, which he took out on A-Ma and me. Anger was his one escape from timidity. He wanted no sympathy for either his dead limb or useless genitals.

Perhaps people find me odd rather than pitiful. I will describe my appearance and let you judge. I am thin but not emaciated and have strong teeth. This latter feature is most unusual for a Hong Kong person of my generation. Many years ago, a dentist courted me. He taught me well about oral hygiene, trained as he had been at an American university. Unfortunately, he was slightly rotund, which offended A-Ba. I think A-Ma wouldn't have minded the marriage, but she always sided with my father, who believed it wise to marry one's own physical type (illiteracy did not prevent him from developing philosophies, as you've already witnessed). I was then in my mid-thirties. After the dentist, there were no other men and, as a result, I never left home, which is our custom for unmarried women and men, a loathsome custom but difficult to overthrow. We all must pick our battles, and my acquiring English, which my parents naturally knew not a word, was a sufficiently drastic defiance to last a lifetime, or at least till they expired.

This dinner at Lutèce has come and gone, and you haven't tasted a thing. It's what happens when we converse over much and do not concentrate on the food. At home, we ate in the silence of A-Ba's rage.

What a shame, but never mind, I promise to share the bounty next time. This meal must have been good because the bill is in the thousands. I pay by traveler's checks because, not believing in debt, I own no credit cards.

Last night's dinner weighs badly, despite my excellent digestion, so I take a long walk late in the afternoon and end up in Chelsea. New York streets are dirtier than I imagined. Although I did not really expect pavements of gold, in my deepest fantasies, there did reign a glitter and sheen.

No one talks to me here.

The air is fetid with the day's leftover heat and odors. Under a humid, darkening sky, I almost trip over a body on the corner of Twenty-fourth and Seventh. It cannot be a corpse! Surely cadavers aren't left to rot in the streets.

A-Ma used to tell of a childhood occurrence in her village. An itinerant had stolen food from the local pig trough. The villagers caught him, beat him senseless, cut off his tongue and arms, and left him to bleed to death behind the rubbish heap. In the morning, my mother was at play, and while running, tripped over the body. She fell into a blood pool beside him. The corpse's eyes were open.

He surely didn't mean to steal, she always said in the telling, her eyes burning from the memory. *Try to forget,* my father would say. My parents specialized in memory. They both remained lucid and clear-headed till they died.

But this body moves. It's a man awakening from sleep. He mumbles something. Startled, I move away. He is still speaking. I think he's saying he's hungry.

I escape. A taxi whisks me back to my hotel, where my table is reserved at the restaurant.

The ceiling at the Oak Room is roughly four times the height of an average basketball player. The ambience is not as seductive as promised by the Plaza's literature. The problem with reading the wrong kind of literature is that you are bound to be disappointed.

This is a man's restaurant, with a menu of many steaks. Hemingway and Fitzgerald used to eat here. Few of my students have heard of these two, and none of them will have read a single book by either author.

As an English teacher, especially one who was not employed at a "name school" of the elite, I became increasingly marginal. Colleagues and friends converse in Cantonese, the only official language out of our three that people live as well as speak. The last time any student read an entire novel was well over twenty years ago. English Literature is not on anyone's exam roster anymore; to desire it in a Chinese colony is as irresponsible as it was of me to master it in our former British one.

Teaching English is little else than a linguistic requirement. Once, it was my passion and flight away from home. Now it is merely my entrée to this former men's club.

But I must order dinner and stop thinking about literature.

The entrées make my head spin, so I turn to the desserts. There is no gooseberry tart! Ever since *David Copperfield*, I have wanted to taste a gooseberry tart (or perhaps it was another book, I don't remember). I tell the boy with the water jug this.

He says. "The magician, madam?"

"The orphan," I reply.

He stands, open-mouthed, without pouring water. What is this imbecility of the young? They neither serve nor wait.

The waiter appears. "Can I help with the menu?"

"Why?" I snap. "It isn't heavy."

But what upsets me is the memory of my mother's story, which I'd long forgotten until this afternoon, just as I hoped to forget about the teaching of English Literature, about the uselessness of the life I prepared so hard for.

The waiter hovers. "Are you feeling okay?"

I look up at the sound of his voice and realize my hands are shaking. Calming myself, I say. "*Au jus*. The prime rib, please, and escargots to start," and on and on I go, ordering in the manner of a man who retreats to a segregated club, who indulges in oblivion because he can, who shuts out the stirrings of the groin and the heart.

I wake to a ringing phone. Housekeeping wants to know if they may clean. It's already past noon. This must be jet lag. I tell Housekeeping, Later.

It's so *comfortable* here that I believe it is possible to forget.

I order brunch from Room Service. Five-star hotels in Hong

Kong serve brunch buffets on weekends. The first time I went to one, Veronica paid. We were both students at university. She wasn't wealthy, but her parents gave her spending money, whereas my entire salary (I was already a working teacher by then) belonged to my parents. The array of food made my mouth water. *Pace yourself*, Veronica said. *It's all you can eat.* I wanted to try everything, but gluttony frightened me.

Meanwhile, A-Ba's voice. *After four or more days without food, your stomach begins to eat itself*, and his laugh, dry and caustic.

But I was choosing brunch.

Mimosa. Smoked salmon. Omelet with Swiss cheese and chives. And salad, the expensive kind that's imported back home, crisp Romaine in a Caesar. Room Service asks what I'd like for dessert, so I say chocolate ice cream sundae. Perhaps I'm more of a bumpkin than I care to admit. My colleagues, former students, and friends would consider my choices boring, unsophisticated, lacking in culinary imagination. They're right, I suppose, since everything I've eaten since coming to New York I could just as easily have obtained back home. They can't understand, though. It's not *what* but *how much.* How opulent. The opulence is what counts to stop the cannibalism of internal organs.

Will that be all?

I am tempted to say, Bring me an endless buffet, whatever your chef concocts, whatever your tongues' desire.

How long till my money runs out, my finite account, ending this sweet exile?

Guest Relations knocks, insistent. I have not let anyone in for three days. I open the door wide to show the manager that everything is fine, that their room is not wrecked, that I am not crazy even if I'm not on the social register. If you read the news, as I do, you know it's necessary to allay fears. So I do, because I do not wish to give the wrong impression. I am not a diva or an excessively famous person who trashes hotel rooms because she can.

I say, politely, that I've been a little unwell, nothing serious, and to please have Housekeeping stop in now. The "please" is significant; it shows I am not odd, that I am, in fact, cognizant of civilized language in English. The manager withdraws, relieved.

For dinner tonight, I decide on two dozen oysters, lobster, and filet mignon. I select a champagne and the wines, one white and one red. Then, it occurs to me that since this is a suite, I can order enough food for a party, so I tell Room Service that there will be a dozen guests for dinner, possibly more. *Very good,* he says, and asks how many extra bottles of champagne and wine, to which I reply, As many as needed.

My students will be my guests. They more or less were visitors during those years I tried to teach. You mustn't think I was always disillusioned, though I seem so now. To prove it to you I'll invite all my colleagues, the few friends I have, like Veronica, the dentist who courted me and his wife and two children, even Kwai-sin and my parents. I bear no grudges; I am not bitter towards them. What I'm uncertain of is whether or not they will come to my supper.

This room, this endless meal, can save me. I feel it. I am vanquishing my fear of death and opulence.

There was a time we did not care about opulence and we dared to speak of death. You spoke of famine because everyone knew the stories from China were true. Now, even in this country, people more or less know. You could educate students about starvation in China or Africa or India because they knew it to be true, because they saw the hunger around them, among the beggars in our streets, and for some, even in their own homes. There was a time it was better *not* to have space, or things to put in that space, and to dream of having instead, because no one had much, except royalty and movie stars and they were *meant* to be fantasy—untouchable, unreal—somewhere in a dream of manna and celluloid.

But you can't speak of famine anymore. Anorexia's fashionable and desirably profitable on runways, so students simply *can't see the hunger.* My colleagues and friends also can't, and refuse to speak of it, changing the subject to what they prefer to see. Even our journalists can't seem to see, preferring the reality they fashion rather than the reality that is. I get angry, but then, when I'm calm, I am simply baffled. Perhaps my parents, and friends and colleagues and memory, are right, that I *am* too stubborn, perhaps even too slothful because instead of *seeing* reality, I've hidden in my parents' home, in my life as a teacher, even though the years were dreary and long, when what I truly wanted, what I desired, was to embrace the opulence, forsake the hunger, but was too lazy to turn the cookie instead.

I mustn't be angry at them, by which I mean all the "thems" I know and don't know, the big impersonal "they." Like a good English teacher I tell my students, you *must* define the "they." Students are students and continue to make the same mistakes, and all I can do is remind them that "they" are you and to please, please, try to remember because language is a root of life.

Most of the people can't be wrong all the time. Besides, whose fault is it if the dream came true? Post-dream is like post-modern; no one understands it, but everyone condones its existence.

Furthermore, what you can't, or won't see, *doesn't* exist.

Comfort, like food, exists, *surrounds* me here.

Not wishing to let anger get the better of me, I eat. Like the Romans, I disgorge and continue. It takes hours to eat three lobsters and three steaks, plus consume five glasses of champagne and six of wine, yet still the food is not enough.

The guests arrive and more keep coming. Who would have thought all these people would show up, all these people I thought I left behind. Where do they come from? My students, colleagues, the dentist and his family, a horde of strangers. Even Kwai-sin and her silly hats, and do you know something, we *do* look a little alike, so Peter Martin wasn't completely wrong. I changed my language to change my life, but still the past throngs, bringing all these people and their Cantonese chatter. The food is not enough, the food is never enough.

Room Service obliges round the clock.

Veronica arrives, and I feel a great relief, because the truth is, I no longer cared for her anymore when all we ate was rice porridge. It was mean-spirited, I was ungrateful, forgetting that once she fed me my first buffet, teasing my appetite. *Come out, travel,* she urged over the years. It's not her fault I stayed at home, afraid to abandon my responsibility, traveling only in my mind.

Finally, my parents arrive. My father sits down first to the feast. His leg is whole, and sperm gushes out from between his legs. *It's not so bad here,* he says, and gestures for my mother to join him. This is good. A-Ma will eat if A-Ba does, they're like that, those two. My friends don't understand, not even Veronica. She repeats now what she often has said, that my parents are "controlling." Perhaps, I say, but that's unimportant. I'm only interested in not being responsible anymore.

The noise in the room is deafening. We can barely hear each other above the din. Cantonese is a noisy language, unlike Mandarin or English, but it is alive. This suite that was too empty is stuffed with people, all needing to be fed.

I gaze at the platters of food, piled in this space with largesse. What does it matter if there *are* too many mouths to feed? A phone call is all it takes to get more food, and more. I am fifty-one and have waited too long to eat. They're right, they're all right. If I give in, if I let go, I will vanquish my fears. *This* is bliss, truly.

A-Ma smiles at the vast quantities of food. This pleases me because she so rarely smiles. She says, *Not like lazy cookie man, hah?*

Feeling benevolent, I smile at my parents. *No, not like him,* I say. *Now, eat.*

ABOUT JOY HARJO

A Profile by William Pitt Root

To say this fine fall morning that Joy is in the air is true: courtesy of KSUT-FM, broadcasting from the Southern Ute Reservation, this startling cut from the CD *Letter from the End of the Twentieth Century,* half-read, half-sung, is one of many by Joy Harjo and her band, Poetic Justice, regularly heard on FM stations serving audiences with large segments of Native Americans and Hispanics throughout the Southwest.

> I'm not afraid of love
> or its consequence of light.
>
> It's not easy to say this
> or anything, when my entrails
> dangle between paradise
> and fear....
>
> —*from "The Creation Story"*

Who else could've written this passage, no less sung it, with that twisting manifestation of polarities Harjo has made one of her trademarks, the disquieting torque of "consequence," the difficulty of speech after evisceration, and the gut connection between paradise and fear? That last bit may be a gritty flip of the medieval concept of that golden chain connecting earth and Heaven, an example of what is implied in her evocative title-phrase *Reinventing the Enemy's Language.*

To hear Harjo perform is to learn there will be no chitchat, no diversion whatsoever; rather, you find you are attending a spirit so sharply focused that it's as if the words on her page, in her heart, must ignite as she reads them. And it is to recognize that the traditional stance she takes as a poet, that of the truth-teller, is assumed without a trace of false modesty. Nothing about her smacks of posturing. She is from that deep vein of upright sayer-singers for whom the stories told are matters of life and death—not for them-

Hulleah Tsinhnahjinnie

selves only, but for their people as well. "My audience," Harjo says, "starts with my tribal nation, spreads out to include those who are also trying to find a way through this particularly rough layer of the world." And she adds, "I hear from them."

Over the past twenty-five years, Harjo has established herself as a courageous and powerful spokesperson for those who are often less heard, particularly America's indigenous peoples. Incorporating Native American myths, spirituality, and imagery into her writing, she has published seven books of poetry, and her honors include the American Book Award, the Delmore Schwartz Memorial Award, the American Indian Distinguished Achievement in the Arts Award, and the Lila Wallace–Reader's Digest Fund Writer's Award. With Gloria Bird, she co-edited the seminal anthology *Reinventing the Enemy's Language: Contemporary Native Women's Writings of North America*, and she has written a book of stories for children, *The Good Luck Cat*.

That Harjo the poet has also become Harjo the singer and Harjo the saxophonist is well-known among her fans, less so among newer readers. Few, however, know that she won prizes for her painting before she wrote or that she has been working in film almost as many years as she's worked in words. Fewer still are aware that she is now training to become competitive at open-sea outrigger-canoeing among the deep blue waters between the islands of Hawaii, where she now lives, commuting to her current job at UCLA, frequently interrupting that schedule to travel around the country, indeed around the world, giving performances with her band as well as individual readings.

All this is a far cry from her childhood in rural Oklahoma after being born the oldest of four children in Tulsa, in 1951, into a family of Muskogee (Creek) and Scots-Irish blood. Song language was her first experience with poetry. "By four years old," she says, "I knew the lyrics to most songs I heard from my mother or the radio or school. The qualities that stood out, that entranced me, were rhythm married with sound sense and meaning. Poems connected with my soul, which was a place that made dense sense." When she was eight, her parents divorced. For a while, she was deeply involved with a local church, first lured there by "vacation Bible school announcements threaded with suckers," she recalls. "I knew there was more candy where that came from, and attended mostly for the coconut cookies and Kool-Aid." Nonetheless, she became devout. She read the Bible three times and organized performances in her neighborhood, giving impassioned sermons. She even thought of becoming a missionary, but left the church, forever, after she witnessed the minister embarrassing two Mexican girls who'd been noisy.

Eventually she left the state to go to boarding school at the Institute of American Indian Arts in Santa Fe, where her talents were appreciated for the first time in an academic setting. "I arrived there barely alive," she says. "I was suicidal. At IAIA I was given permission to be an Indian artist. I was given permission to be human. That was no small thing." Like her great-aunt and grandmother, both reputable artists, Harjo intended to become a painter. She began to change her mind as she read and heard such "poet warriors" as Audre Lorde and Gwendolyn Brooks, Galway Kinnell and Richard Hugo (in whom she was quick to appreciate "the shine of his compassion"). Also indelible were the examples of Neruda and Okot p'Bitek, the great Ugandan dramatic poet. All of those influences upon her were ultimately galvanized by connection with Native American writers like Leslie Marmon Silko (Laguna) and Simon Ortiz (Acoma Pueblo) who read at the

Institute. Other inspirations were N. Scott Momaday (Kiowa), James Welch (Blackfeet), Roberta Hill (Oneida), and Vi Hilbert (Lushootseed), the storyteller/scholar from whom Harjo says she learned both dignity and "a truth with knowledge beyond small human understandings."

At the University of New Mexico as an undergraduate, Harjo devoted herself to becoming a poet; she has tirelessly worked ever since to augment Muscogean traditions with European and African lyric and narrative forms. And yet in certain poems, as Leslie Ullman shrewdly noted in *The Kenyon Review,* Harjo's stance has not been so much "representative of a culture as it is the more generative one of a storyteller whose stories resurrect memory, myth, and private struggles that have been overlooked, and who thus restores vitality to the culture at large." Harjo herself adds another layer of involvement, the dead themselves, in her poem "Resurrection," about the massacre at Esteli, near the Honduran-Nicaraguan border:

> We all watch for fire
> for all the fallen dead to return
> and teach us a language so terrible
> it could resurrect us all.

Harjo has consistently identified poetry as a literal method of survival. "I don't believe I would be alive today," she has explained, "if it hadn't been for writing. There were times when I was conscious of holding on to a pen and letting the words flow, painful and from the gut, to keep from letting go of it all." Again and again she credits imagination (access to spiritual perspectives) and art (the craft that enables one to recreate that access) as tools that enable her continuously to resurrect herself from her own ashes.

She has had her share of challenges. In high school, she became pregnant with her son, Phil. In 1968, she moved from Santa Fe back to Oklahoma, scraping together a living from various jobs, including a stint as a nurse's assistant at a hospital. In 1973, her daughter, Rainy Dawn, was born, and Harjo—practically destitute, trying to get through college, work, take care of her kids, and contend with their alcoholic, abusive father—"shivered to a breakdown, an earthquake of the heart," a state of terror so paralyzing it was "difficult even to swallow, and each step had to be calculated" to move at all. She managed, nonetheless, to earn her undergraduate degree at the University of New Mexico in 1976 and then her M.F.A. from the University of Iowa in 1978. A series of visiting lectureships led in 1985 to an assistant professorship at the University of Colorado. She then taught for two years at the University of Arizona, where she pulled triple-duty in the Women's Studies, Creative Writing, and Native American Studies departments. Next came six years as full professor at her alma mater, the University of New Mexico. Most recently, of course, she has moved to Honolulu. Throughout, her reputation as a poet has steadily spread and strengthened. She published her first book, *What Moon Drove Me to This*, in 1980, and three years later she broke through with her second volume, *She Had Some Horses*. Still in print like most of her subsequent work, it is widely used in literature courses.

During her career, she has steadily intensified her efforts to contain language in ever more musical forms, to make it go, like music alone, straight to the heart with as little mediation as possible. Her reading voice more and more resembles a singing voice, with musical phrasing; her 2004 CD, *Native Joy for Real*, is a vigorous exploration of a far wider variety of alternating, cross-cutting styles than any of her earlier recordings. In some cuts, like "Fear Song," Harjo and her musicians have come up with a combination of instruments and styles so harrowingly effective as to be quite unlike anything else. Other cuts have hints of hip-hop as well as jazz or blues or reggae. One piece, "The Had-It-Up-to-Here Round Dance," is a dialogue between a man and woman, both Native American, struggling with their reactions as each sees the other in the arms of a sequence of partners, including whites. It could easily derail, but, dead-on and deadly as it is, it's also amusing, funny because we see ourselves being ridiculous in the figures of others.

When Harjo says, "I was born with eyes that never close," she describes an unwavering condition of witness—a curse or a blessing, depending upon how one regards it and what one does with it. In Native American belief, the regard given to vision is similar: it is one's sacred task, having seen, to share. Harjo proclaims, "I feel strongly that I have a responsibility to all the sources that I am: to all past and future ancestors, to my home country, to all places that I touch down on and that are myself, to all voices, all women, all of my tribe, all people, all earth, and beyond that to all beginnings and endings.... [Writing] frees me to believe in myself, to be able to speak, to have voice, because I have to."

In 1989, at the conclusion of Bill Moyers's interview with Harjo for his *The Power of the Word* PBS series, he seemed mesmerized by her image of herself as "memory alive." On his face appeared that slightly goofy, beatific grin perfected earlier during his classic interviews with Joseph Campbell, and Moyers declared, "That's what you really are, you know, *memory alive.*" And he beamed at her. She ducked her head ever so slightly, as she tends to do when given a direct compliment, before she replied, also smiling, "That's what we all are."

ZACHARIS AWARD *Ploughshares* is pleased to present Mark Turpin with the fourteenth annual John C. Zacharis First Book Award for his collection of poems, *Hammer* (Sarabande, 2003). The $1,500 award—which is named after Emerson College's former president—honors the best debut book by a *Ploughshares* writer, alternating annually between poetry and fiction.

This year's judge was the poet John Skoyles, who is a *Ploughshares* trustee. In choosing the collection for the Zacharis Award, he said: "Mark Turpin's *Hammer* focuses on a man's occupation in a blow-by-blow account of what it's like to work with your hands, and to live with men who do the same. These poems rise to that occasion by maintaining a balance between their burly subjects and musical language. Turpin's enormous skill lets him wrest from this rough world the heart and soul of workingmen, their families, their labors, and their rest. By concentrating on his subjects with rigor and imagination, the poems resound beyond the day-to-day, and engage matters of life and death. *Hammer* is a moving collection, spoken in a voice marked by strength and warmth."

Mark Turpin was born in Berkeley, California, in 1953, and grew up mostly in Livermore, a Bay Area bedroom community populated half by ranchers and half by nuclear physicists who worked at the weapons laboratory. His father was a Presbyterian minister, his mother a schoolteacher. In 1969, the family moved back to Berkeley, their first day coinciding with the riot at the People's Park, where James Rector was shot by the police.

At Berkeley High School, Turpin decided he wanted to become a writer. "I had a great English teacher/actor who introduced Shakespeare to us—with all its violence and bawdiness and ambiguity," Turpin says. "I think the intellectual action of crossing over into a more comprehensive understanding of Shakespearean language, that feeling of the intervening centuries disappearing, was the catalyst for my passion. It is paradoxical that the same teacher who inspired me to love literature also advised me that I was not eccentric enough to be a writer. It's true—I was a fairly sweet, anxious, good-hearted boy. I felt terribly ordinary and longed for distinction."

After graduating high school, he attended Feather River College, a junior college in the Sierras, but never obtained a bache-lor's degree. He got married at nineteen,  had two children, and worked as a carpen-ter. In 1985, he was invited to audit Robert Pinsky's graduate writing workshop at Berkeley. His first publication was in *The Paris Review* in 1987. It wasn't until 1999, however, that he went to the graduate writ-ing program at Boston University for his master's.

Asked how *Hammer* came about, Turpin writes: "I was mainly just engaged in the process of writing poems. I wrote a poem about construction that worked, and so, I wrote another one. The writing of the book took many years, too many to number in public. For a while it was to be a book half-devoted to construc-tion; in fact, many of the poems in it still are only peripherally related to construction work. Once I recognized the theme, I took it on as if it were a rehabilitation, a recovery of an undocumented life—but mainly it was a vocabulary of images and actions I was familiar with, a way to get at feelings and ideas more universal."

Turpin is still working as a carpenter, but he functions more as a contractor now, his clients mainly artists, architects, and poets. He is writing poems for a new book and developing a one-man performance piece loosely based on the material in *Hammer*. He has also been teaching poetry privately. "I love to teach," he says. "I'd like to do it exclusively, since I've spent twenty-five years earning my bread as a carpenter. I've paid my dues. I'd rather stay fit going to the gym."

smith, Elaine Markson, James Alan McPherson, Grafton Nunes, and John Skoyles.

SUBSCRIBERS Please note that on occasion we exchange mailing lists with other literary magazines and organizations. If you would like your name excluded from these exchanges, simply send us a letter or e-mail message stating so. Our e-mail address is pshares@emerson.edu. Also, please inform us of any address changes with as much advance notice as possible. The post office usually will not forward bulk mail.

No Planets Strike, *poems by Josh Bell* (Zoo): The network of motifs in Josh Bell's debut volume, *No Planets Strike,* create as intricate a system as the roads, tunnels, and bridges that comprise the transportation systems of major metropolitan cities, allowing the reader to traverse the speaker's psyche at dizzying, gratifying speeds. This is not a book for the agoraphobic, the acrophobic, or the erotophobic: Bell's fierceness of wit, his deft lyricism, his ability to swing adroitly between dictions high and low, combine to create a world that is savage and irreverent, yet fraught with longings spiritual and corporeal. One senses the engaged presence of the poet throughout this book, as the consequences of love gone bad accumulate like the wreckage of a freeway pile-up during rush hour. —*Cate Marvin*

What You've Been Missing, *stories by Janet Desaulniers* (Iowa): Janet Desaulniers's debut collection, which won the John Simmons Short Fiction Award, is surprisingly lovely and thrilling, in that it offers incredible intimacy and honesty in the face of life's worst calamities. In one story, a mother notes after the death of her young son: "Life, no longer ordinary, becomes profligate—a reckless boil of mute, mystifying details." Throughout the book, all of the protagonists, each with his or her own compelling brand of integrity, are challenged into becoming "suddenly interested again in what things mean." This resonant collection forces its characters and readers to confront the moments when ordinary life ceases to exist. Only then do they begin to understand what they've been missing. —*Fred Leebron*

The Man Who Sleeps in My Office, *poems by Jason Sommer* (Chicago): Jason Sommer's latest book is tough and nuanced, at turns both public and private, and ambitious in the subjects it takes on: while touring a concentration camp in Prague, a young American couple think of "[t]hose who were naked here / and had their flesh reft from them suddenly" as they make love furtively in the outlying woods; a man purchases a mynah bird to keep his sick wife company, and then must listen when it "turns impressionist" after she's passed away. A poet primarily concerned with ethics, Sommer boldly asks his reader: "Say a writer imagines something horrible / for a character . . . who is the author of the eventual deed?" —*Cate Marvin*

George Garrett recommends *The Stone That the Builder Refused,* a novel by Madison Smartt Bell: "The magnificent final volume of Bell's Haitian trilogy about the only successful slave revolution in history. Epic in scope, yet grounded and richly detailed, this huge work is a masterpiece." (Pantheon)

Mary Gordon recommends *Ideas of Heaven,* stories by Joan Silber: "This original, finely wrought collection deals with spiritual issues, always with a combination of grace and lightness." (Norton)

DeWitt Henry recommends *Garrett in Wedlock,* stories by Paul Mandelbaum: "In this 'novel-in-stories,' Garrett, who feels 'himself to be without ethnic heritage,' is thrown into a jumble of heritages by love of his wife and her two children by earlier marriages, one to a Norwegian adventurer, the other to an Indian bigamist. The Norwegian comes to live with them as he dies from mad cow disease. When Garrett visits India with his stepdaughter, he is challenged by meeting the birth father, and later by her conversion to Islam and insistence on an arranged marriage. Overall, Mandelbaum presents a rich cross section of contemporary family life, ruled by chaos theory and by genuine love. 'It baffled Garrett, how people ended up the way they did'—in this case, whole, and in the family's heart." (Berkley)

Maxine Kumin recommends *Horses and the Human Soul,* poems by Judith Barrington: "The poem, Barrington writes, 'has lodged in my heart like a stone in the shoe.' It is a perfect image for recollection. Here are the horses of her English childhood and the outbreak of World War II filtered through family reminiscence, her coming of age, the disastrous marriage, and her self-acceptance as a lesbian. Her voice is lyrical, her intelligence palpable throughout this book." (Story Line)

Philip Levine recommends *From the Meadow,* selected and new poems by Peter Everwine: "This collection presents all of Everwine's poems that he still regards with affection in a career that spans forty years or more, many of the poems never collected before. It includes a few of his remarkable translations from the Hebrew as well as some of his interpretation of Nahuatl poems. For me the true gems are his own poems, which are like no other in our language: they possess the simplicity and clarity I find in the great Spanish poems of Antonio Machado and his contemporary Juan Ramon Jiminez but in contemporary American English and in the rhythms of our speech, that rhythm glorified. He presents us with poetry in which each moment is recorded, laid bare, and sanctified, which is to say the poems possess a quality one finds only in the greatest poetry." (Pittsburgh)

Margot Livesey recommends *Maps of the Imagination: The Writer as Cartographer,* nonfiction by Peter Turchi: "I love the layering of imagery and information that Peter Turchi accomplishes as *Maps of the Imagination* unfolds. The illustrations throughout are wonderful—so surprising and various and interesting. My brain felt enlarged by reading this account of so many different possible journeys." (Trinity)

Joyce Peseroff recommends *Letters to Jane,* correspondence by Hayden Carruth: "While researching Jane Kenyon's papers archived at the UNH library, I came across a file of letters written to her by Hayden Carruth during the long months of her illness. Carruth didn't expect a reply; he didn't write to be cheery or tell her to keep her chin up. Instead, he described ordinary days ignited by the 'luminous particular' Jane so valued, creating meditative, sharp, and sometimes hilarious scenes in an intimate voice I couldn't stop reading. Now others can share Carruth's moving chronicle of common life and the power of friendship." (Ausable)

Robert Pinsky recommends *Will in the World: How Shakespeare Became Shakespeare,* a biography by Stephen Greenblatt: "To recommend a bestseller? Strange in a way, but *Ploughshares* readers should know that Greenblatt is a real writer. Unlike many a 'noted scholar' he writes wonderful sentences and paragraphs. Here is a book about a literary writer that is fun to read. Greenblatt rises above any distinction between narrative and understanding." (Norton)

EDITORS' CORNER

*New Books by
Our Advisory Editors*

Russell Banks, *The Darling,* a novel: Set in Liberia, Banks's riveting new book explores the interrelated history of race problems in the U.S. and Africa. (HarperCollins)

Madison Smartt Bell, *The Stone That the Builder Refused,* a novel: Bell gives us the final, climactic novel in his glorious trilogy about Toussaint Louverture. (Pantheon)

James Carroll, *Crusade: Chronicles of an Unjust War,* essays: Carroll collects his searing, passionate *Boston Globe* columns about the Bush administration's "coercive unilateralism." (Holt)

Rita Dove, *American Smooth,* poems: In her eighth superb collection, Dove pays homage to the grit and mother wit that inform our mongrel cultural heritage. (Norton)

Stuart Dybek, *Streets in Their Own Ink,* poems: In his second poetry collection, Dybek finds extraordinary vitality in the same vibrant imagery that animates his celebrated fiction. (FSG)

George Garrett, *Double Vision,* a novel: As expected from the ever-inventive Garrett, this novel is a witty tour de force, marrying fact and fiction about a gifted generation of American writers. (Alabama)

Gish Jen, *The Love Wife,* a novel: Jen, in her most exuberant and accomplished book, provides a brilliant portrait of a new "half-half" American family. (Knopf)

Bill Knott, *The Unsubscriber,* poems: The poems in Knott's collection, his first in a decade, are surreal yet vernacular, outrageous yet tender—absolutely unique, iconoclastic, and astonishing. (FSG)

Yusef Komunyakaa, *Taboo,* poems: In the first book of a trilogy, Komunyakaa shows that he is our great poet of connectivity—the secret blood that links slave and master, explorer and native, stranger and brother. (FSG)

Philip Levine, *Breath,* poems: Levine, in these heady, extraordinary new poems, looks back at his life to unearth rites of passage in an America of victories and betrayals. (Knopf)

Margot Livesey, *Banishing Verona,* a novel: A shy housepainter and a pregnant radio show host begin an affair in Livesey's radiant, delicious new novel, and then they're immediately separated, setting them off in transatlantic pursuit. (Holt)

Campbell McGrath, *Pax Atomica,* poems: With singular verve, McGrath continues ever deeper into the jungle of American culture with poems that are musical, comedic, and impassioned. (Ecco)

Robert Pinsky, *An Invitation to Poetry,* anthology: Pinsky and co-editor Maggie Dietz's compelling compilation of poems is accompanied by quotations from Favorite Poem Project participants, along with a DVD. (Norton)

Christopher Tilghman, *Roads of the Heart,* a novel: In Tilghman's generous and powerful novel, a man and his father—a former Maryland senator—journey on the road and discover the resilient truths of their family. (Random)

Richard Tillinghast, *Poetry and What Is Real,* essays: Sure to be a seminal work, Tillinghast's engaging book discusses British and American modernists such as Yeats and Auden and neglected masters like John Crowe Ransom. (Michigan)

Derek Walcott, *The Prodigal,* poems: Walcott presents another masterwork that is a journey through physical and mental landscapes, a sweeping yet intimate epic. (FSG)

Alan Williamson, *The Pattern More Complicated,* poems: Williamson's verse from the last three decades are collected with new poems that beautifully draw his *oeuvre* together. (Chicago)

CONTRIBUTORS' NOTES

Winter 2004–05

CHRIS ABANI is the author of the novels *GraceLand* and *Masters of the Board* and the poetry collections *Kalakuta Republic, Daphne's Lot,* and *Dog Woman.* A Middleton Fellow at the University of Southern California, he teaches in the M.F.A. program at Antioch University and is a visiting assistant professor at the University of California, Riverside.

AI is the author of seven books of poetry, including *Dread* (Norton, 2003) and *Vice* (Norton), which won the 1999 National Book Award. She is a full professor at Oklahoma State University and is currently working on a memoir about her family of Native Americans, Irish, Scots-Irish, and mulatto people in Texas and Oklahoma.

ELLEN BASS's most recent book, *Mules of Love* (BOA Editions), won the Lambda Literary Award for Poetry. Among her other awards are the *New Letters* Prize, the Larry Levis Prize from *The Missouri Review,* and a Pushcart Prize. She teaches poetry and creative writing in Santa Cruz, California. See www.ellenbass.com.

RICK BASS is the author of twenty books of fiction and nonfiction, most recently *Caribou Rising.* In 2005, Houghton Mifflin will publish his new novel, *The Diezmo.* He is a board member of the Yaak Valley Forest Council, the Montana Wilderness Association, and various other environmental groups. He lives with his family in northwest Montana.

BRUCE BOND's most recent collections of poetry include *Cinder* (Etruscan, 2003), *The Throats of Narcissus* (Arkansas, 2001), and *Radiography* (BOA Editions, 1997). Presently he is Professor of English at the University of North Texas and Poetry Editor for *American Literary Review.*

MELANIE CESSPOOCH is an enrolled member of the Northern Ute Tribe, Whiterocks, Utah. She graduated with her B.F.A. in Creative Writing from the Institute of American Indian Arts, Santa Fe, New Mexico. Currently she is working on a poetry manuscript and is employed as a lab technician at the IAIA.

MARILYN CHIN is the author of *Dwarf Bamboo* and *The Phoenix Gone, The Terrace Empty.* Her latest book, *Rhapsody in Plain Yellow,* was published by Norton in 2002. She has won numerous awards for her poetry, including a Radcliffe Institute fellowship from Harvard and two NEA fellowships. She co-directs the M.F.A. program at San Diego State University.

EDDIE CHUCULATE (Creek/Cherokee) is from Muskogee, Oklahoma. He has published stories in *Weber Studies, Many Mountains Moving,* and *The Iowa Review,* and has a story forthcoming in the Winter 2004 edition of *Manoa.* A

Stegner fellow at Stanford University from 1996–98, he now lives in Albuquerque, where he is a copy editor and columnist at *The Albuquerque Tribune.*

SANDRA CISNEROS was born in Chicago in 1954, the third child and only daughter in a family of seven children. Her books include two poetry books, *My Wicked Wicked Ways* and *Loose Woman;* a collection of stories, *Woman Hollering Creek;* a children's book, *Hairs/Pelitos;* and two novels, *The House on Mango Street* and *Caramelo.* She lives in San Antonio, Texas.

JAN CLAUSEN has new poems out or forthcoming in *Bloom, Fence, The Hat, Margie,* and *The North American Review.* The recipient of a 2003 NYFA Poetry Fellowship, she teaches at Eugene Lang College and in Goddard College's M.F.A. writing program. Her most recent book is *Apples and Oranges,* a memoir.

ALLISON HEDGE COKE is the author of two poetry collections, *Off-Season City Pipe* and *Dog Road Woman,* winner of the 1998 American Book Award, and a memoir, *Rock, Ghost, Willow, Deer.* "Ghost Deer" is from her forthcoming book of poetry with photographs of Indigenous mound sites critically endangered in the far eastern end of the Great Plains. She teaches in the M.F.A. program at Northern Michigan University.

BRENDAN CONSTANTINE's collection *Hyenas 57* was a finalist for the National Poetry Series. His work has appeared in *ArtLife, The Cider Press Review,* and *Abalone Moon,* among other journals. He teaches poetry at The Windward School in Los Angeles.

JON DAVIS, Creative Writing Chair at the Institute of American Indian Arts, is the author, most recently, of the screenplays *Gift of the Condor* and *Catamount Falls,* and a play, *Anna Without Angels.* Poems by heteronyms appear in *Hanging Loose, Blue Mesa, Luna, Obsidian, American Letters & Commentary, Tar River, poemmemoirstory, Calyx,* and *The Muse Strikes Back.*

RON DE MARIS is a Miami poet. His work has appeared in many magazines, including *Poetry, The New Republic, The Nation, APR, The Sewanee Review, The Southern Review, The Antioch Review, The Gettysburg Review, New England Review,* and more. His book-length manuscript, *The Architect of the Infinite,* is in search of a publisher.

CHARD DENIORD is the author of three books of poetry, *Asleep in the Fire* (Alabama, 1990), *Sharp Golden Thorn* (Marsh Hawk, 2003), and *Night Mowing* (Pittsburgh, 2005). His poems and essays have appeared recently in *The American Scholar, New England Review, The Pushcart Prize, Best American Poetry,* and elsewhere. He teaches at Providence College and directs the low-residency M.F.A. program at New England College.

VALERIE DUFF is the coordinator of PEN New England. Her poems have appeared in *Denver Quarterly, P.N. Review, Salamander,* and elsewhere, and she has received individual artist grants from the Massachusetts Cultural Council and the St. Botolph Foundation. She completed her M.Phil. in Creative Writing at Trinity College, Dublin, in 2002.

MARTÍN ESPADA's seventh poetry collection, *Alabanza: New and Selected Poems, 1982–2002* (Norton, 2003), received a Paterson Award for Sustained Literary Achievement and was named an American Library Association Notable Book. Another collection, *Imagine the Angels of Bread* (Norton, 1996), won an American Book Award. He teaches at the University of Massachusetts–Amherst.

MONICA FERRELL is a Wallace Stegner fellow at Stanford University and a past "Discovery"/*The Nation* prizewinner. Her poems are forthcoming in *Slate, The New York Review of Books,* and *Denver Quarterly.*

JENNIFER FOERSTER is a graduate of the Institute of American Indian Arts in New Mexico, where she currently lives. She has published in *Tribal College Journal* and *Red Ink Magazine,* and has been the recipient of the Ataa'xum Fellowship at Dorland Mountain Arts Colony. She also makes ceramic sculpture.

JAVIER F. GONZALEZ was born in 1976 in Bogotá, Colombia. Primarily a visual artist, he received his B.A. in Fine Arts in 1998, then moved to study in Italy, New York, and finally Santa Fe, New Mexico, where he began his studies as a creative writer. He writes poetry and essays on painting and art theory.

JENNIFER GROTZ is the author of *Cusp* (Houghton Mifflin, 2003), winner of the Bakeless Prize and the Texas Institute of Letters Natalie Ornish Prize. Her translations of La Tour du Pin's psalms received an award from the American Translators Association and appear in *New England Review, Center, Lyric,* and elsewhere.

DONALD HALL has published fifteen books of poems, including *Without, Old and New Poems, The One Day,* and, most recently, *The Painted Bed.* In 2003, he published a book of short stories, *Willow Temple,* and *Breakfast Served Any Time All Day,* new and selected essays on poetry. *The Best Day, The Worst Day,* a memoir of his life with Jane Kenyon, will appear in April 2005.

JEFF HARDIN teaches at Columbia State Community College in Columbia, Tennessee. His poems have appeared in *Iron Horse Literary Review, Mid-American Review, Poem, West Branch,* and elsewhere. He is the author of two chapbooks, *Deep in the Shallows* and *The Slow Hill Out.* His first collection, *Fall Sanctuary,* received the Nicholas Roerich Poetry Prize from Story Line Press and will appear in December 2004.

TRAVIS HOLLAND's stories have previously appeared in *Glimmer Train, Five Points,* and *The Quarterly.* A graduate of the University of Michigan, where he recently received his M.F.A., he lives in Ann Arbor with his wife, Amy, and their son, Aidan. He is currently working on a novel.

MAXINE KUMIN's fifteenth poetry collection, *Jack and Other New Poems,* will be published in January 2005. Her awards include the Ruth E. Lilly Poetry Prize and the Pulitzer Prize. She served as Consultant in Poetry to the Library of Congress in 1980–81. She and her husband live on a farm in central New Hampshire.

ALEX KUO just completed residencies at Bellagio on a Rockefeller Foundation grant and at Knox College as Distinguished-Writer-in-Residence. His most recent book, *Lipstick and Other Stories* (the title story appeared in *Ploughshares* Vol. 26/4), received the American Book Award.

PATRICE DE LA TOUR DU PIN (1911–1975) was best known in France for the three-volume multi-genred work entitled *Une Somme de poésie,* and several shorter books of poetry, including *Psaumes de tous mes temps,* which collects the psalms he wrote and revised throughout his life.

JOSÉ F. LACABA has published five collections of poetry in Tagalog, but it is his work as freelance journalist, screenwriter, editor, translator, and university lecturer that pays the bills. His screenplay credits include Filipino films that have been shown at various international film festivals, including Cannes, Berlin, and Toronto.

HARRIET LEVIN's first book of poems, *The Christmas Show,* was the winner of a Barnard New Women Poet's Prize and the Alice Fay di Castagnola Award. Recent work appears in *Denver Quarterly, The Iowa Review, The Kenyon Review,* and *Pennsylvania English.* She directs the Writing Program and the Honors Concentration in Creative Writing at Drexel University.

YIYUN LI came to the U.S. from China in 1996 and began to publish in English in 2002. Her fiction and essays have appeared in *The New Yorker, The Paris Review, The Gettysburg Review,* and elsewhere. Winner of the first Plimpton Prize for New Writers, she is currently an M.F.A. candidate at the Iowa Writers' Workshop. Her first book, a collection called *The Princess of Nebraska,* will be published in 2005.

CHIP LIVINGSTON's poetry has been published recently in *Brooklyn Review, Apalachee Review, Cimarron Review,* and *Stories from the Blue Moon Café, Volume 3.* His fiction has appeared previously in *Ploughshares,* as well as in *Rosebud, Crazyhorse, Blithe House Quarterly,* and other journals. He lives in New York City.

ADRIAN C. LOUIS has taught in the Minnesota State University system since 1999. He has written several books of poems and fiction, including the novel *Skins,* which was produced as a feature film in 2002.

JEREDITH MERRIN is the author of two collections of poetry, *Shift* (1996) and *Bat Ode* (2001), both from the University of Chicago Press. Her essay on John Clare appears in the most recent issue of *The Southern Review.* Her new poetry manuscript is entitled *Mon Age.*

DAN NAMINGHA was born in 1950 in Keams Canyon, Arizona, and now lives in Santa Fe, New Mexico. He studied art at the University of Kansas in Lawrence, the Institute of American Indian Arts in Santa Fe, and the American Academy of Art in Chicago. His work has been included in over fifty exhibitions and may be found in museum collections in the U.S., Germany, England, and Slovakia. See www.namingha.com.

ALICIA OSTRIKER has published ten volumes of poetry, including *The Crack in Everything* and *The Little Space,* both National Book Award finalists. A new book,

No Heaven, is due this spring. Her most recent prose volume is *Dancing at the Devil's Party: Essays on Poetry, Politics, and the Erotic.*

ELISE PASCHEN is the author of *Infidelities,* winner of the Nicholas Roerich Poetry Prize, and *Houses: Coasts.* Her poems have been published in *The New Republic, Poetry, The New Yorker,* and in numerous anthologies. She is co-editor of *Poetry in Motion, Poetry in Motion from Coast to Coast,* and *Poetry Speaks.*

LUCIA PERILLO's fourth book of poems, *Luck Is Luck,* will be published soon. Her poetry and prose have appeared in many small magazines, and earned her a MacArthur fellowship in 2000. She lives in Olympia, Washington.

JOSÉ EDMUNDO OCAMPO REYES was born and raised in the Philippines. He holds an M.F.A. in writing from Columbia University.

DAVID ROMTVEDT's past books of poetry include *Certainty* (White Pine) and *A Flower Whose Name I Do Not Know* (Copper Canyon), a selection of the National Poetry Series. His recordings with the Fireants are *Bury My Clothes* and *Ants on Ice.* He is the current poet laureate of the state of Wyoming.

WILLIAM PITT ROOT's first book, *The Storm and Other Poems* (Atheneum, 1969), will be republished in a facsimile edition in 2005; he will also have a chapbook of new work coming out from Carolina Wren Press. Having traveled in Sweden and Prague this past summer, he confesses his delight with recently having left teaching to resume writing full-time.

JESS ROW's first collection of stories, *The Train to Lo Wu,* will be published by the Dial Press in January 2005. His work has appeared in *The Best American Short Stories 2001* and *2003* and *The Pushcart Prize XXVI.* He lives in New York City and is an assistant professor of English at Montclair State University.

CATHIE SANDSTROM's work has appeared in *Solo, Lyric, Cider Press Review,* the anthologies *Matchbook* and *So Luminous the Wildflowers,* and is forthcoming in *Runes.* A two-time winner in the Lannan Foundation's Poetry in the Windows, she has lived in Japan, England, Denmark, the Deep South, the Carolinas, and Appalachia. She now makes her home in Sierra Madre, California.

PHILIP SCHULTZ's latest book is *Living in the Past* (Harcourt, 2004). *The Holy Worm of Praise* came out in 2002. His work has won the Levinson Prize from *Poetry,* the Lamont Prize, an award from the American Academy of Arts and Letters, and a National Book Award nomination. He directs The Writers Studio in New York City.

REBECCA SEIFERLE's third poetry collection, *Bitters* (Copper Canyon, 2001), won the 2002 Western States Book Award and a Pushcart Prize. Her translation of Vallejo's *The Black Heralds* was published by Copper Canyon Press in late 2003. She will be Jacob Ziskind poet-in-residence at Brandeis for 2004–05.

REGINALD SHEPHERD is the editor of *The Iowa Anthology of New American Poetries,* which was published this past fall by the University of Iowa Press. He is the author of four books of poetry, including *Otherhood* (Pittsburgh, 2003) and

Some Are Drowning (Pittsburgh, 1994), winner of the 1993 AWP Award. He lives in Pensacola, Florida.

QUENTIN SHERWOOD received a B.A. from Kalamazoo College and an M.F.A. from Warren Wilson College. His poems have appeared in *Alaska Quarterly Review, New Letters,* and *Dunes Review.* He and his wife resided in Michigan. An accomplished athlete, musician, and painter, he worked as a newspaper reporter, kayaking instructor, and carpenter. He was killed while bicycling in September 2002. He was forty years old.

CATHY SONG is the author of *Picture Bride, Frameless Windows, Squares of Light, School Figures,* and *The Land of Bliss.* She lives with her family in Honolulu.

GARY SOTO's forthcoming books include a young adult short story collection, *Help Wanted* (Harcourt, 2005), and a book of middle-grade poems, *Worlds Apart: Traveling with Fernie and Me* (Putnam, 2005).

GERALD STERN recently published a small book of sayings, or petite narratives, called *Not God After All* (Autumn House). His next book of poems, *Everything Is Burning,* will be released by W.W. Norton in the spring of 2005. He lives in Lambertville, New Jersey.

MARC J. STRAUS has two collections of poetry, *One Word* (1994) and *Symmetry* (2000), both from *TriQuarterly*–Northwestern University Press. "Alchemy" is from a new set of doctor poems, which together with his patient poems are being staged Off-Broadway in the production *Not God* and will be published by Northwestern in 2005. He runs a medical oncology practice in New York.

ROBERT SULLIVAN belongs to the New Zealand Maori tribe Nga Puhi. He has written four poetry books, a graphic novel, and a children's book, and won many New Zealand awards. He works as Assistant Professor of English at the University of Hawai'i, Manoa. See www.nzepc.auckland.ac.nz./authors/sullivan/.

ARTHUR SZE is the author of *The Redshifting Web: Poems 1970–1998* and *The Silk Dragon: Translations from the Chinese.* A new collection of poems, *Quipu,* will be published in 2005 by Copper Canyon Press. He lives in Santa Fe and teaches at the Institute of American Indian Arts.

LAURA TOHE is Diné (Navajo). She authored *Making Friends with Water* and the award-winning *No Parole Today,* and co-edited *Sister Nations: Native American Women Writers on Community.* She writes essays, stories, and children's plays that have appeared in Canada and Europe, and is Associate Professor of English at Arizona State University.

ALPAY ULKU's first book, *Meteorology* (BOA Editions, 1999), was selected as an "Exciting Debut" by the Academy of American Poets. Poems from his second manuscript are in recent issues of *Ploughshares, The Malahat Review, Atlanta Review, Hayden's Ferry Review, Crazyhorse,* and *Canary Review.* He works as a technical writer in Chicago.

PAMELA USCHUK is the author of the award-winning *Finding Peaches in the*

Desert and *One Legged Dancer*. Her work has appeared in over two hundred journals and anthologies worldwide. Her forthcoming book is *Scattered Risks* (Wings). She directs the Salem College Center for Women Writers.

G. C. WALDREP's first book, *Goldbeater's Skin*, won the 2003 Colorado Prize for Poetry, as well as a Greenwall grant from the Academy of American Poets. His work has appeared recently in *Colorado Review, New American Writing, Ninth Letter, Quarterly West, American Letters & Commentary*, and other journals. Currently he divides his time between North Carolina and Iowa.

CHARLES HARPER WEBB's most recent book of poems, *Tulip Farms and Leper Colonies*, was published in 2001 by BOA Editions. He edited *Stand Up Poetry: An Expanded Anthology*, which was published by the University of Iowa Press in 2002. Recipient of grants from the Whiting and Guggenheim foundations, he teaches at California State University, Long Beach.

ORLANDO WHITE is Diné (Navajo) from Sweetwater, Arizona. His clans are of the Zuni Water Edge People and born from the Mexican Clan. He is currently a creative writing student and holds an A.A. degree from the Institute of American Indian Arts in Santa Fe, New Mexico.

NANCE VAN WINCKEL's fourth collection of poetry is *Beside Ourselves* (Miami, 2003). She has received two NEA poetry fellowships. New poems appear in *The Gettysburg Review, Agni*, and elsewhere. She has also published three books of short fiction, most recently *Curtain Creek Farm* (Persea, 2000). She teaches in the M.F.A. programs at Eastern Washington University and Vermont College.

SCOTT WITHIAM's poems have appeared or are forthcoming in *Field, Tar River Poetry, Sonora Review, 5 A.M., English Journal, Blue Mesa Review, The Marlboro Review, The Florida Review, Puerto del Sol*, and *Drunken Boat*. His first book, *Arson and Prophets*, was published by Ashland Poetry Press in the fall of 2003.

XU XI is the author of several books, including the novels *The Unwalled City* and *Hong Kong Rose*. She also co-edited *City Voices*, an anthology of Hong Kong writing in English. She currently teaches at Vermont College's M.F.A. program, and lives somewhere between New York, Hong Kong, and New Zealand. See www.xuxiwriter.com.

∾

GUEST EDITOR POLICY *Ploughshares* is published three times a year: mixed issues of poetry and fiction in the Spring and Winter and a fiction issue in the Fall, with each guest-edited by a different writer of prominence, usually one whose early work was published in the journal. Guest editors are invited to solicit up to half of their issues, with the other half selected from unsolicited manuscripts screened for them by staff editors. This guest editor policy is designed to introduce readers to different literary circles and tastes, and to offer a fuller representation of the range and diversity of contemporary letters than would be possible with a single editorship. Yet, at the same time, we expect every issue to reflect our overall standards of literary excellence. We liken

Ploughshares to a theater company: each issue might have a different guest editor and different writers—just as a play will have a different director, playwright, and cast—but subscribers can count on a governing aesthetic, a consistency in literary values and quality, that is uniquely our own.

~

SUBMISSION POLICIES We welcome unsolicited manuscripts from August 1 to March 31 (postmark dates). All submissions sent from April to July are returned unread. In the past, guest editors often announced specific themes for issues, but we have revised our editorial policies and no longer restrict submissions to thematic topics. Submit your work at any time during our reading period; if a manuscript is not timely for one issue, it will be considered for another. We do not recommend trying to target specific guest editors. Our backlog is unpredictable, and staff editors ultimately have the responsibility of determining for which editor a work is most appropriate. Mail one prose piece or one to three poems. No e-mail submissions. Poems should be individually typed either single- or double-spaced on one side of the page. Prose should be typed double-spaced on one side and be no longer than thirty pages. Although we look primarily for short stories, we occasionally publish personal essays/memoirs. Novel excerpts are acceptable if self-contained. Unsolicited book reviews and criticism are not considered. Please do not send multiple submissions of the same genre, and do not send another manuscript until you hear about the first. *No more than a total of two submissions per reading period.* Additional submissions will be returned unread. Mail your manuscript in a page-size manila envelope, your full name and address written on the outside. In general, address submissions to the "Fiction Editor," "Poetry Editor," or "Nonfiction Editor," not to the guest or staff editors by name, unless you have a legitimate association with them or have been previously published in the magazine. Unsolicited work sent directly to a guest editor's home or office will be ignored and discarded; guest editors are formally instructed not to read such work. *All manuscripts and correspondence regarding submissions should be accompanied by a business-size, self-addressed, stamped envelope (S.A.S.E.) for a response only. Manuscript copies will be recycled, not returned.* No replies will be given by e-mail or postcard. Expect three to five months for a decision. We now receive well over a thousand manuscripts a month. Do not query us until five months have passed, and if you do, please write to us, including an S.A.S.E. and indicating the postmark date of submission, instead of calling or e-mailing. Simultaneous submissions are amenable as long as they are indicated as such and we are notified immediately upon acceptance elsewhere. We cannot accommodate revisions, changes of return address, or forgotten S.A.S.E.'s after the fact. We do not reprint previously published work. Translations are welcome if permission has been granted. We cannot be responsible for delay, loss, or damage. Payment is upon publication: $25/printed page, $50 minimum and $250 maximum per author, with two copies of the issue and a one-year subscription.

THE NAME *Ploughshares* 1. The sharp edge of a plough that cuts a furrow in the earth. 2a. A variation of the name of the pub, the Plough and Stars, in Cambridge, Massachusetts, where the journal *Ploughshares* was founded in 1971. 2b. The pub's name was inspired by the Sean O'Casey play about the Easter Rising of the Irish "citizen army." The army's flag contained a plough, representing the things of the earth, hence practicality; and stars, the ideals by which the plough is steered. 3. A shared, collaborative, community effort. 4. A literary journal that has been energized by a desire for harmony, peace, and reform. Once, that spirit motivated civil rights marches, war protests, and student activism. Today, it still inspirits a desire for beating swords into ploughshares, but through the power and the beauty of the written word.

Cover art from the painting
Symbolism VI
by Dan Namingha
Acrylic on canvas, 40˝ x 50˝, 2004
Courtesy of Niman Fine Art

NATIONAL
ENDOWMENT
FOR THE ARTS

massculturalcouncil.org

BENNINGTON WRITING SEMINARS

MFA in *Writing and Literature*
Two-Year Low-Residency Program

A. BLAKE GARDNER

FICTION
NONFICTION
POETRY

Partial Scholarships Available
For more information contact:
Writing Seminars, Box PL
Bennington College
One College Drive
Bennington, VT 05201
802-440-4452, Fax 802-440-4453
www.bennington.edu

MARGIE

THE AMERICAN JOURNAL OF POETRY

The Robert E. Lee & Ruth I. Wilson
Poetry Book Award Contest

POSTMARK DEADLINE : JAN. 15 , 2005

First Prize: **$2,500**

& Publication of the Winning Book
Plus 100 Complimentary Author's Copies

Finalist Judge: **Billy Collins**

SPECIAL NOTE: An INTRODUCTION to the Winning Book
will be Written by Mr. Collins.

GUIDELINES: 1) Manuscripts must be typed, single or double-spaced, and consecutively numbered. Submit between 48-64 pages of poetry. 2) Include a cover page (with author's name, address, phone & title of manuscript) & a second title page (with no bio info.) Include an acknowledgements page listing poems previously published in periodicals. 3) Include an entry fee check for $25 payable to MARGIE, Inc. for each manuscript submitted. Simultaneous submissions are acceptable. Please notify Intuit House immediately if your manuscript is accepted for publication elsewhere. Your cancelled check will serve as receipt for your manuscript. 4) Include a self-addressed, stamped envelope (SASE) to receive notification of contest results. No manuscripts can be returned. All manuscripts will be considered for publication. 5) Mail entries by POSTMARK DEADLINE OF JAN. 15, 2005 to: Intuit House, c/o MARGIE, POB 250, CHESTERFIELD, MO 63006-0250.
Questions? Email us at margiereview@aol.com.

Series Editor: Robert Nazarene / *Senior Editor:* James Wilson

Intuit House Poetry Series
An imprint of *Margie / The American Journal of Poetry*

A portion of each entry fee will be donated to our contest beneficiary:
FEED THE CHILDREN

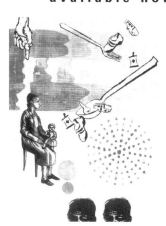

45th Annual
Best Poem Contest

www.stlouispoetrycenter.org

POSTMARK DEADLINE: FEBRUARY 15, 2005

FIRST PRIZE: $2,000

For Best Poem
and publication in *Margie / The American Journal of Poetry*

SECOND PRIZE: $250   **THIRD PRIZE: $100**

Finalist Judge:
DENISE DUHAMEL

GUIDELINES: 1) Submit 3 unpublished poems along with a $15 entry fee payable to The St. Louis Poetry Center (60 line limit per poem). 2) Additional poems may be submitted for $5 each add'l poem. 3) Enclose a single sheet with your name, address, phone & the title of each poem. Please, no names on poems themselves. 4) All poems will be considered for publication in *Margie*. Simultaneous submissions are acceptable. 5) Entries must be POSTMARKED BY FEB. 15, 2005. 6) Mail entries to: THE ST. LOUIS POETRY CENTER, 567 NORTH & SOUTH RD., #8, ST. LOUIS, MO 63130. Only send copies. Poems will not be returned. Please send a Self-Addressed Stamped Envelope for contest results.

June 27-July 22, 2005 • 19th Year

New York State
Summer Writers Institute
Workshops in fiction, poetry, non-fiction

AT SKIDMORE COLLEGE, SARATOGA SPRINGS, NEW YORK

Teaching Faculty

Fiction
MARY GORDON • RICK MOODY • MARGOT LIVESEY
DARRYL PINCKNEY • HOWARD NORMAN • JAY MCINERNEY
LEE K. ABBOTT • BINNIE KIRSHENBAUM • AMY HEMPEL
ANDREA BARRETT • ELIZABETH BENEDICT • JULIA SLAVIN

Poetry
FRANK BIDART • ROSANNA WARREN
HENRI COLE • APRIL BERNARD

Non-Fiction
PHILLIP LOPATE • JAMES MILLER

Visiting Faculty
MICHAEL ONDAATJE • JOYCE CAROL OATES • ROBERT PINSKY
MICHAEL CUNNINGHAM • ANN BEATTIE • RUSSELL BANKS
LOUISE GLÜCK • ROBERT STONE • CHARLES SIMIC
FRANCINE PROSE • RICHARD HOWARD • JAMAICA KINCAID
WILLIAM KENNEDY

Writers-in-Residence
offering private tutorials on novel and non-fiction manuscripts

FICTION: TONY EPRILE • DARIN STRAUSS • GREG HRBEK
NON -FICTION: SAMANTHA DUNN

For brochure
please email: cmerrill@skidmore.edu
or write: Chris Merrill • Special Programs
Skidmore College • Saratoga Springs, NY 12866
Phone: 518 580 5590
Web: http://www.skidmore.edu/administration/osp/summer_writers_institute/index.htm

THE
*Rona
Jaffe*
Foundation
WRITERS' AWARDS

Celebrating Ten Years

*The Rona Jaffe Foundation identifies and
supports emerging women writers.
Recipients receive awards of $10,000.*

2004 WINNERS

Carin Clevidence
(fiction)

Ann Harleman
(fiction)

Dana Levin
(poetry)

Michele Morano
(nonfiction)

Tracy K. Smith
(poetry)

Sharan Strange
(poetry)

Announcing Joy Harjo's new CD
Native Joy for Real

"*Native Joy for Real* marks Joy Harjo's debut as a singer/songwriter, an album so strong, so brimming with soul and beauty, that even longtime fans will be astonished by the power of its poetic vision. Harjo has created ten singular invocations of contemporary life, on and off the reservation, that deal with the joys and tribulations of everyday existence. The music blends traditional Native rhythms and singing with jazz, rock, blues, and a touch of hip-hop. Harjo's trademark intensity is still inspiring. The songs feature memorable refrains, smoky sax work, subtle powwow-based beats, and uplifting lyrics. The unifying factor is Harjo's poetic and political vision."

—J. Poet, music editor of *Native Peoples* Magazine

For more information or to purchase a CD, visit
Joy Harjo's website at www.joyharjo.com

Ploughshares

Stories and poems for literary aficionados

Known for its compelling fiction and poetry, *Ploughshares* is widely regarded as one of America's most influential literary journals. Each issue is guest-edited by a different writer for a fresh, provocative slant—exploring personal visions, aesthetics, and literary circles—and contributors include both well-known and emerging writers. In fact, *Ploughshares* has become a premier proving ground for new talent, showcasing the early works of Sue Miller, Mona Simpson, Robert Pinsky, and countless others. Past guest editors include Richard Ford, Derek Walcott, Tobias Wolff, Carolyn Forché, and Rosellen Brown. This unique editorial format has made *Ploughshares*, in effect, into a dynamic anthology series—one that has established a tradition of quality and prescience. *Ploughshares* is published in trade paperback in April, August, and December: usually a fiction issue in the Fall and mixed issues of poetry and fiction in the Spring and Winter. Inside each issue, you'll find not only great new stories and poems, but also a profile on the guest editor, book reviews, and miscellaneous notes about *Ploughshares*, its writers, and the literary world. Subscribe today.

Read thousands of works online for free: www.pshares.org